RAISING THE BAR

RAISING THE BAR

A LAWYER'S MEMOIR

By

RUTH RYMER

MILL CITY PRESS

Mill City Press, Inc.
2301 Lucien Way #415
Maitland, FL 32751
407.339.4217
www.millcitypress.net

Paperback ISBN-13: 978-1-6628-3204-8
Hard Cover ISBN-13: 978-1-6628-3205-5
Ebook ISBN-13: 978-1-6628-3206-2

TABLE OF CONTENTS

ACKNOWLEDGMENTS

M any people and organizations have helped with *Raising the Bar*.

I appreciate everyone's assistance.

My arms and legs for this publication was Stephanie Barko, Literary Publicist.

I thank Heidi M. Thomas, editor, and award-winning author of the Cowgirl Dreams book series, and

Sandi Corbitt-Sears for her patience and insight as my final editor.

Thanks to Gina Logan for putting me at ease in front of her camera.

For rethinking my front cover, I appreciate book designer Rebecca Lown.

Gratitude for production goes to my team at Salem Author Services, including but not limited to Logan Mungo.

Thanks to Barbara Singer for her service as my personal consultant.

And lastly, I thank my soul mate in our quests for our doctorates, Kay Talbot, Ph.D.

For my children, Nevin Lane Miller
and Stefani Joan Miller

WHAT IS MY NAME?

My parents named me

PATRICIA RUTH RYMER

They called me PATSY, which I respelled PATSI.
Sherwin tried to soften it by calling me PATTY.
It didn't work, so I dropped anything related to PATRICIA
And became

RUTH MILLER

Under that name, I practiced law for over thirty years.
Then I claimed the best of all names:

RUTH RYMER

PREFACE

M any years ago, I flew to the Midwest on a trip that gave me an opportunity to visit my brother, John, and his family. We would be meeting in person for the first time since I married Sherwin.

After dinner, John brought up my break with the family. He asked, "What was the fight between you and Mom and Dad really about? I never heard your side, and they never talked about it."

I sighed. At last, someone wanted to hear the truth of what happened from me. "They liked Sherwin until they discovered he was Jewish. Then they ordered me to break off our relationship. I refused, and they expelled me from the family. The argument was about anti-Semitism. Anti-Semitism was wrong then. It is wrong now. It was wrong at the beginning of time. It will be wrong at the end of time."

John, who had become an ophthalmologist, looked at me for several minutes and said, "I think I understand. Your position is that marrying a Jewish man caused them to throw you out of the family, to disown you."

"Yes, that's exactly what happened."

His wife, a neurologist, frowned. "There must have been something else. The director of my medical group is Jewish. He's been in his position for thirty years. Sherwin being Jewish is such a trivial matter."

I shrugged. "I'm only sure of what they told me at the time. I don't understand anything else about their reaction."

John said, "I've never really gotten it either. But if what they told you was the real reason, was marrying Sherwin worth the price you paid?"

That is the question. Let me tell you, my readers, what really happened.

SECTION 1:

GAINING A HUSBAND AND LOSING A FAMILY

CHAPTER ONE

Sherwin Miller was so strikingly handsome that he brought tears to my eyes—six feet two inches tall, a full head of dark hair, and perfect features. He wore a tweed sports coat with dark trousers, making him by far the best-dressed man at the event. When he asked me to dance, my knees became weak.

I'd spent my freshman year at Mills College. I knew it was a women-only institution. However, I was told that men often visited the campus. I hadn't exactly gone to college to get a "Mrs. Degree," which was a common practice in 1950, but I was certainly looking for a husband.

I wanted more of what were then thought of as social norms, including the classic husband in the workforce and wife at home. A career in music would fit that norm perfectly. I could accompany soloists, play the organ in church, or perhaps venture into my own solo practice. Music was everything to me. When I married, it could only be to a man who would want for me—and for us—what I wanted for myself: a traditional marriage with additional purpose and meaning.

When no men appeared on the Mills College campus for dating purposes that year, I transferred to the University of Colorado. The welcome dance sponsored by my new sorority provided an opportunity to mingle with the opposite sex.

With Sherwin, I experienced love at first sight. We found something to giggle about immediately. It felt as if he had been part of my soul from birth. Although I had not been born Jewish, so many of my girlfriends were Jewish that I felt Jewish in my heart and soul.

When I visited their homes, I met warm, happy, centered families with scholarly interests and a charming sense of humor. They accepted me, but some of their warmth cooled after I faced the inevitable question: "Patsi, are you Jewish?" I always regretted having to answer, "No."

In general, I felt happier with my Jewish friends' families than with my own. They had characteristics my parents lacked.

Sherwin also possessed qualities I admired. He was headed for medical school and had enrolled in psychology classes to determine whether he wanted to become a psychiatrist.

Interesting, fun-loving friends dominated his social life. Surprisingly, he had formed a close friendship with his philosophy professor, who taught a summer-session course. We met her husband, and our friendship with the couple continued after we left Colorado.

Sherwin's best student friend was a World War II veteran who often shared his experiences. That friend, along with several colleagues, once played a silly joke on Sherwin, placing a dying houseplant on his bed with this dedication:

This withered plant
Upon the bed
Reminds us of
Dear Miller's head.

When Sherwin and I saw it in his college room, we both laughed and laughed. Humor had not been a part of my life before I met Sherwin. Knowing him changed everything. Soon I became part of a foursome, going out with Sherwin's friend and his date.

So much in my life felt exciting, and discussions with Sherwin topped the list. He was an intellectual, and I wanted to be an intellectual. We talked about philosophy, history, literature, and politics. When we were together, I felt complete and happier than I had ever been.

Sherwin and I did not spend that Christmas together, as it was a family occasion in my household. In addition to my brother, John, who arrived on Halloween ten years after my birth, I had two sisters: Betty, born on Mother's birthday in 1938 and Anne, born on Dad's birthday in 1944. Our six-foot Christmas tree was covered with unique decorations and surrounded by an impressive number of gifts.

Shortly after Christmas, Sherwin introduced me to his parents. His gray-haired father stood six feet tall, and his charming and outgoing personality made me feel welcome immediately. Sherwin's mother was tiny, only five feet, one inch tall. With dark, naturally bouffant hair, exquisite clothing, and an amiable personality, she made quite an impression on me. I considered both of his parents delightful.

Early in our relationship, Sherwin and I talked about a future together. I made it clear I wanted to continue my studies. He responded that we would both attend school. If necessary, we would alternate years. One year, he would be in school while I worked. The next year, we would reverse.

He said, "I'd be just as happy seeing you in school as I would be to attend myself."

I had never experienced such happiness. Sherwin was perfect.

CHAPTER TWO

It was time for Sherwin to meet my parents. I believed Dad held me in high esteem, and I had no trepidation about how he would view my new boyfriend. Sherwin seemed closer to my estimation of what Dad might like than any other man I had dated. My father hadn't liked many. He dismissed them as too fat, too thin, too strange, or not much of a man. His negative comments about several racial or cultural groups told me they were also off the list, including Negroes, Catholics, Jews, Italians, and foreigners. I had learned to ignore or sidestep Dad's prejudices just as I accommodated both his atheism and Grandmother Reinhardt's religiosity.

The first meeting, a Sunday dinner at our family home in Denver, proved successful. I knew my parents liked Sherwin because they welcomed him warmly. He appeared to like them as well. Sherwin also met Grandmother Rymer, my two younger sisters, and my brother. Everyone got along, and the general conversation centered on family.

When Dad talked directly to Sherwin, however, they discussed medical school. Dad didn't think Sherwin's psychology classes would help him, as the medical establishment approached mental illness differently than did the psychological establishment. Sherwin explained his desire to understand the subject matter before making a lifetime commitment to it. Dad appeared satisfied that Sherwin was on the right track for a career as a doctor.

My mother received a Ph.D. in biochemistry from the University of Colorado Medical School in 1935 and became the director of the Belle Bonfils Memorial Blood Bank, housed in a campus building with other medical facilities. She knew the dean of the medical school well and gained more prominence in her field than Dad had in his. He'd served as acting director for the Colorado Psychiatric Hospital during World War II and then went into private practice.

When you met my parents as a couple, however, she behaved as a traditional wife rather than the CEO of a significant medical entity. She hid her accomplishments, which included her degrees and noteworthy executive position within the community.

Mother met Sherwin a second time, just after he and I had gone skiing. The three of us enjoyed a cordial conversation, and the future of our relationship appeared promising.

A short time after that meeting, I attended the usual Sunday family dinner on my own. When Sherwin's name came up in conversation, my parents' remarks indicated delight and approval. Then I made an offhand statement about Sherwin that revealed he was Jewish. The tone of the discussion abruptly shifted from sunshine and blue skies to thunder and lightning.

My father said, "You cannot continue to see him. Your association with the man will lower our standing in the community."

Astonished, I ignored his tone, which suggested finality. "Why?" I asked. "You have Jewish friends and a close association with at least one Jewish psychiatrist."

"Oh, Harry is only about a quarter Jewish, and his wife is Christian."

I sighed, thinking, *Harry Steinberg is clearly Jewish.*

Father continued. "Both Mother and I worked our way through school, and we've worked hard to raise our family to a high social standing. My practice depends on attracting upper-class patients. Having a Jewish son-in-law would destroy us."

Anger rose up in me, but I never argued with my parents. I stared at Dad; my objection silent: *I don't think so. Your outspoken prejudices are much more likely to do that.*

Dad's face turned red as he talked. When he took a step toward me, I wondered if he intended to hit me, so I veered to the side.

"We will not let you lower our standing in the community! I will not finance you with one more dollar if you marry him. If you marry him, I will disown you! Do you understand me?"

I let my thoughts play out in my mind without voicing them. *Dad, you don't own me. What you are saying is impossible. You're making so many ridiculous threats.*

I took a deep breath and said calmly, "No one has yet talked about marriage. I'll consider what you said, but now I need to get back to the university. As you may remember, I am in summer school. I'd like to concentrate on that."

I returned to Boulder, feeling annoyed. I'd contemplated changing my piano performance major to music education and engaged with my professors in substantial coaching and evaluation about the issue. They reminded me that few jobs would be available in what I initially wanted to do, but many existed in the field of teaching. Although switching my major to music education would be a compromise, I could find a position in a public or private school. With that decision behind me, I felt a little more settled in my future career plans.

When I told Sherwin about my parents' attitude, he said, "I just don't believe it. I can't imagine that's what they really think. There must be another reason. The founders of your father's profession, Freud and Jung, were Jewish. Jewish psychiatrists are common. Your father couldn't get along in his profession with such a vehement anti-Semitic attitude."

"I agree. If what you say is true, having a Jewish son-in-law would not lower their standing in the community, but spouting anti-Semitism would surely do it."

"Absolutely! I don't know what their problem is."

Collectively, we sighed. I had never seen my parents so emotional and irrational about anything, but I refused to take their reaction seriously. My life was mine to live, and I couldn't support an old-fashioned, morally bankrupt philosophy.

We left it at that.

CHAPTER THREE

One afternoon a month later, Sherwin proposed marriage. My excitement battled with awareness
of my parents' attitude, so I told him I would have to think
about it. He said he understood.

I did give it a lot of thought. The next time Sherwin and I
met, I took a deep breath and said, "There may be an element
of truth in the concerns my parents have about Dad's career. I
talked with them after your proposal, and their position is the
same as before."

"About my being Jewish?"

"Yes. When I talked to Mother, she said, 'Dump him.' Dad
reiterated that he would disown me if I marry you." I bit my lip.

He said, "It can't be because I'm Jewish. It must be something else. He won't disown you. That would make no sense."

"You're probably right. Even so, I'm worried. I think we
should go underground. I'll tell them we've broken up. I'll
be in my junior year next fall. If I go to summer school, I can
graduate at the end of the year. Then I can get a job teaching."

I saw the frown on his face, but I continued. "You have one
more year as an undergraduate before you can start medical

school. By then, it won't matter if they don't want us to get married. They can't stop us. In the meantime, I'll take another man home and pretend to be interested in him. They will take the pressure off if they think I've let you go."

Sherwin took my hand in his and stared into my eyes. "Patty, I love you. I've told my parents many times that if I ever find a girl I want to marry, I will never let her go. I will never let you go."

I began to cry. "My darling, I love you so much."

Squeezing my hand tightly, he said, "If we can't get married now, I couldn't stand pretending we aren't together. It would be dishonest. I'll leave. I'll transfer to UCLA, stay with family there, and go to medical school in California."

I needed clarity, so I asked for more time to think about it. He sat quietly, letting me consider the options.

My mind would not accept the possibility of losing Sherwin. *How can I lose him? He is my soul mate. He is the part of me I didn't think I could ever find, a man I can love as much as I love Sherwin. I cannot risk spending my life without him.*

I walked around the room, continuing to ruminate. *We are intellectuals. I could never find another man like him. My parents will not carry out their threats. Never. We could marry and give them time to get over it.*

After an hour, I sat next to him and said, "Yes, Sherwin, I will marry you."

He embraced me and said, "Wonderful! We'll be so happy."

We planned to marry in late July, following the first session of summer school. We would honeymoon in August and be back in school by September.

Sherwin found a doctor to do a premarital exam and fit me with birth control. We wouldn't need it until after the wedding, because in 1950 only fools engaged in sexual relations before they were married. We might be plunging into unknown waters, but we weren't utterly stupid about it.

The knowledge I'd gained from reading my dad's textbook on obstetrics and gynecology (which I'd done at the age of thirteen) had been useful. I knew when I wanted a family, and I certainly knew how to start one. I also knew how not to have a child before I was ready.

We told Sherwin's parents about our engagement right away. Their response was loving and supportive, the opposite of my parents' reaction. Although it made them sad that my mother and father objected, they still approved of our plans to marry.

Sherwin bought me a half-carat diamond engagement ring set with tiny diamonds on either side of the main stone. I felt ecstatic. Our future was settled at last.

Nothing could stop us from being together.

CHAPTER FOUR

The second Sunday in June erupted in an inferno. The afternoon was not what we had hoped for and not what we expected. Before the family dinner, we announced our engagement, and I showed Mother my engagement ring.

"You can't keep it," she ordered. "Give it back."

My jaw dropped, and I thought, *Mother, don't be absurd. I'm a grown woman.* Her demand disoriented me; I could not grasp what was happening. I'd listened to my parents' threats, but I never imagined they might act on them.

The next hour rehashed the same theme: "We cannot put up with this. Having a Jewish son-in-law will lower our standing in the community. I—I mean we—will disown you if you marry this man." Their nasty behavior surpassed anything I had ever seen from them. I was astonished!

My heart beat erratically, and my stomach clenched. Occasionally, I'd had to put up with their idiosyncrasies, but I thought I had learned to manage them. I was wrong.

Sherwin and I remained quiet but resolute. We sat and simply listened. Finally, Sherwin said, "Dr. Rymer, this is about something other than my being Jewish. As Patsi's father, you surely know you can never hope to marry her yourself."

My mind registered total shock. *Where did Sherwin get that idea?*

It was a defining moment. Defining moments were simply that. They defined the future course of my life.

Dad grabbed Sherwin, who stood two inches taller and was in much better physical condition. Sherwin could easily have bested Dad if he had tried. He didn't try. He went limp. Dad dragged my fiancé to the front door, shoved him through it, and slammed it closed.

"Now," he said, "we can talk to our daughter."

My eyes widened in horror, and my mind raced.

That's it. My father has some sort of abnormal sexual attraction to me. Maybe he didn't know it himself and substituted anti-Semitism. It explains why he hasn't liked any of my boyfriends. Now, faced with my intention to marry Sherwin, he knows he will lose me as a sexual object. Mother is threatened by it. She must think she has no choice other than to take a position as vehement as his. It means I can never get away. I will never be allowed to make my own choices. They will never let me live my own life, and I certainly will not be allowed to marry.

After half an hour, Sherwin rang the doorbell. When my father answered the door, Sherwin took one step inside and asked, "Patty, are you coming with me?"

"Yes," I said, and we left.

That evening, Sherwin wrote a five-page letter to my parents, asking them to change their views and accept him and us as we were. It was more scholarly than they, even with their doctorates, could—or were willing to—comprehend. Because they couldn't understand it, they couldn't respond. The letter follows:

Dear Dr. and Mrs. Rymer,

I am writing to you to both clarify and relieve your minds of the concern that you are expressing in regard to Patsi and myself. While I am deeply involved in this entanglement, I shall try to be objective in everything I say.

In attempting to present the overall picture, a brief resume of a few past events will be beneficial. Patsi has told me that up until the time you learned of my being Jewish, you both "liked and were quite impressed" with me. It was not necessary for her to tell me so, for the visits we had together indicated both feelings of friendship and warmth. Mrs. Rymer, I shall never forget the evening that you, Patsi, and I spent after our skiing trip. It was one of the most memorable and enjoyable talks I have ever had. At that time I was under the impression that you knew of my background, and your kindness and sincerity led me to believe that it made little or no difference to you.

Several weeks later, Patsi told me that she had just mentioned my background to you and that your whole attitude towards me was changed by this knowledge. I must admit that upon hearing this, I was quite stunned. You see, both because of Patsi and because of my liking for the two of you, I wanted very much for you to like me.

Patsi has also told me that you have made your position of disapproval apparent at every given opportunity and that she has tried but has been unable to present either our viewpoint or the facts or the situation to you.

In fairness, I would like to explain several things to you at this time.

In retrospect, I would [*sic*]to first review a few things relating to my background. Since the religious aspect seems to be the idea of greatest concern, let us look at this now. Patsi has told you that I am Jewish, but this is true only when qualified. As you know a clear distinction exists between race and religion, and anthropology indicates that there is no "Jewish race, hence, a person is Jewish only if he believes in and follows the principles of the Jewish Religion. I do admit that for various reasons the Jewish people have remained a close knit group, and have consequently come to be considered as a race, but this fits practical purposes quite well.

It should now be made clear that I have never been closely connected with the group, and from the age of fourteen on, I have had no associations with them. Why? Because the religion and its implications did not satisfy either my spiritual needs or my social needs, and Patsi pointed out that your religious affiliations do not satisfy you. I then attempted to find some religious group that would, and I made an investigation of all the religious groups that I had access to. After several years of searching, I was unable to decide upon a group, and I finally realized that my spiritual needs were being satisfied in the mere appreciation of our universe and its many wonders, while my social needs found satisfaction in having a select group of friends. Max Steiner expresses this idea quite beautifully:

> The unfree denizen of the wilderness does not feel the fetters which bind the man of culture: he thinks the latter enjoys greater freedom. In the measure that I acquire greater freedom, I create new limits and new problems for myself.

I deeply feel that man's whole life shows one continual need: to find himself, to understand himself, and this can only be accomplished by maintaining ones [*sic*] individuality and reacting to situations as an individual and not as a predetermined pattern of ideas.

Dr. Rymer, Patsi has told me of many of your admirable accomplishments. She said that in your attempt to better and further yourself in our society, you worked your way through school. She has also mentioned that you have continued working by penetrating deeper and deeper into your field to further your understanding of the complexities of the human mind, but can you honestly say, Sir, that you have given yourself a chance to understand me?

You asked Patsi earlier some questions that I shall now attempt to answer. You asked, "why can't he be satisfied with what he has? And "what can my daughter offer him that Mr. Ginsberg's daughter can't?" In answering the first, I would like to point out that if Sigmund Freud had been satisfied to remain persecuted for having been born a Jew, he would never have developed his theory of psychoanalysis and modern psychiatry might still be in its infant stages. If Einstein had been satisfied with classical mechanics, nuclear and modern physics would still be underdeveloped.

If you had been satisfied to remain alone, uneducated, and untrained, would you be happy now? And if I were satisfied, life would cease to be worth living ... all I can say is that Patsi offers me every quality I have ever searched for, but I would like to point out that if Patsi were Mr. Ginsberg's daughter, or Mr. Smith's daughter or Mr. Jones' daughter, my feeling toward her would be the same, but Patsi is your daughter, Sir, and I am very glad that she is.

With your permission, I would like to tell you a little more about myself and my plans for the future. As you probably know, I expect to receive my degree next year in mathematical physics and I have done honors work in this field. I am an active member of Pi Mu Epsilon (national honorary mathematics fraternity). After graduation I plan to continue my academic career by entering the field of medicine where I someday hope to put my present training in mathematics to practical use in neurology and psychiatry. To date, I have been accepted into one medical school.

Please understand that I respect you position in this matter. I know your main concern is Patsi and her happiness. Patsi has told me that you pointed out that we would become victims of social ostracization. I would like to interpret the argument from two standpoints. First of all, both of us have at the present time many close friends from all realms of our society. Secondly, we shall continue to maintain these friends and make new friends as time goes on. Nevertheless, you do have a point; for undoubtedly, we shall meet people who shall refuse to take us for what we are, but who in the world would want those people for friends in the first place?

I would now like to tell you about Patsi and myself. I do this believing that the world will always welcome people who are in love, and Patsi and I love each other. This is my justification in attempting to persuade you to re-examine your position. I cannot hope for you to cast off a life-time idea, but I must ask that you at least regard me as an individual and evaluate me in that light. There is one last thing that I must say: for Patsi's sake, please relax your pressure, and realize that her happiness means more to me than anything in this world.

I remain sincerely yours,
SHERWIN U. MILLER

My father addressed only one sentence of the letter and said to me, "He wrote me a letter asking me to take off the pressure."

In the next month, my parents accelerated their position by bringing many other people into the matter. They telephoned the dean of men at the university and asked him to stop our marriage. The dean then called me into his office and told me Sherwin was delinquent on a loan. A few days later, the dean called to apologize. He said the payment had been made on time but had not been posted immediately. The dean later chatted with Sherwin, and then the three of us met. He, like Harry Steinberg, found our story to be nearly incredible. The dean became a close friend, and we corresponded with him for many years.

I asked my closest friend, Marilyn Nelson, to give me a wedding shower. My parents were acting like jerks, but we didn't need to do so. Marilyn told her father, who called mine. "My God," Mr. Nelson was reported to have said. "How awful. I pray that will never happen to me." Marilyn did not call me, but the shower was clearly off. I did not speak to her again for decades.

Mother and Dad visited Sherwin's parents, who lived in a one-bedroom apartment near the state capitol. His father was an engineer for the government, and his mother worked in retail. We heard the story later from Mr. and Mrs. Miller.

Mr. Miller invited my parents into their home and extended pleasantries. After they were seated, Mrs. Miller said, "Will you have some coffee? I picked up a cake this afternoon; may I serve you some?"

"No. No!" my father bellowed. "We're just here to get this thing stopped." It appeared he had nothing more substantive to say.

Sherwin's father did not respond. In my estimation, he was too much of a gentleman to demand that they leave. Mrs. Miller articulated her position by saying, "We would have preferred that Sherwin marry someone of his own faith, but I'll tell you this: if this marriage goes through, I'm not going to commit suicide."

I learned that my father totally misinterpreted her comment. He thought she had agreed with him and lamented that she could not commit suicide. Instead, she meant to belittle him for his rudeness and for making such a big issue out of something so insignificant.

When I heard about my father's shameful rudeness, I wondered how he and Mother could have spouted their obvious anti-Semitism in a Jewish home, especially when they had been so graciously accepted.

Sherwin and I went to see Harry Steinberg and told him all the details of the problem. He was astonished. I wanted to know more about his background, so I said, "Dad says you aren't Jewish. Is that right?"

He smiled and replied, "Technically, he is right. My father was Jewish but not my mother. Under Jewish law, a person must have a Jewish mother to be considered Jewish, but I doubt your dad knows that. Anyway, he and I have never talked about it, and he's always been a mentor to me. I've never heard anything from him like the anti-Semitism you're describing."

He seemed to think about the matter for a moment. Turning to his wife, he asked, "What did you think about my being Jewish or not?"

The two appeared to be happy together. Without hesitation, she said, "I have never even given it a thought."

I looked down at my hands.

Then Dr. Steinberg made a suggestion. "What would happen if you just sat with your father and let him tell you how very badly he feels about this?"

I said, "I wish that would work, but I don't think it will. I've never really had an opportunity to do so. Our discussions involve him telling me what damage I'm going to do to them. He then makes threats about what he'll do to me if I proceed with my plans. I've not been able to have any conversations about any other aspects in this matter. He just yells at me."

Dr. Steinberg shook his head in amazement. "It is hard to believe. I wish you good luck. We hope it turns out okay for you both."

CHAPTER FIVE

On July 17, 1951, Mother and Dad came to my dorm late at night, waking me and my roommate. Dad pulled me out of bed and demanded that I descend to the first floor living room. He refused to even let me put on my robe.

They ordered me to sit on a sofa and stood over me to continue their reign of terror, in full view of anyone passing by, for over an hour. When they finally let me go, I heard someone in the hall comment, "They'd better be careful. Those kids will simply run away and get married."

Both Sherwin and I had taken a calm and cautious approach to my parents' highly charged emotions, but the uncharacteristically raw and vicious behavior I experienced that night appalled me. In the space of a few seconds, my low gear rocketed into overdrive. Lightning struck, earthquakes shook, and Armageddon appeared just over the hill.

But Armageddon was not over a hill; it existed in the Colorado mountains. Our family knew those mountains well. After my twelfth birthday, the three of us spent large portions of every summer there. The fifty-two mountains that towered fourteen-thousand-feet high or more were known as "fourteeners."

My first fourteener was Snowmass. Sometimes the three of us climbed together; at other times, we joined a group of members from the Colorado Mountain Club.

By the time I turned sixteen, I had climbed forty four-teeners and was due to go with Mom and Dad to complete their remaining four. However, I had returned from California the day before we were to leave, and I didn't think I could comfortably go from sea level to fourteen- thousand feet so quickly. When I declined to accompany them, they expressed their disappointment.

My parents had tickets to the opera in the mountains the Sunday after their shocking confrontation at my dorm. I became increasingly nervous about attending. Many what-ifs ran through my mind as I imagined how that trip could become my Armageddon. Dad might pull off the road at a viewpoint and say, "Patsi, look! The place where I proposed to your mother is in the valley below. Come and see it."

When Dad pushed Sherwin through the front door a few weeks earlier, he demonstrated a willingness to use physical force to get his way. I couldn't help but wonder if he would be just as willing to use violence with me. I envisioned him pulling off at a lookout, getting out of the car, and saying to Mother, "Stay here a minute, dear. I'll be right back."

After I followed him to the edge of the cliff, he would put his arm around me and point down to the bottom. I would see nothing but rocks, and he would say, "Oops. I made a mis-take." Then, as he pulled away from me, he would nudge me over the edge.

The rangers would find me dead at the bottom of the cliff, and Dad would be just horribly sorry that he hadn't been able to stop me when I stepped too close to the edge. He could get away with it too. As experienced mountaineers, we knew deaths frequently occurred when a person accidentally slid down the steep terrain. He would be the only witness, and he and Mother would be grieving the tragic death of their beloved daughter. No district attorney would even think of prosecuting such a prominent psychiatrist in his grief, especially one who so often testified in their favor.

Was I being paranoid? Probably. That was not the issue. The issue I faced was whether I would be allowed to control my own life.

I still didn't understand my parents' vehement position about Sherwin. I knew it couldn't be due entirely to anti-Semitism. Maybe it stemmed, in part, from the semi-sexual issue Sherwin raised when he stated that Dad could never marry me. His assertion made some sense because Mother soon became as uncompromising as he had been from the beginning. By siding with Dad, she proved her allegiance to him. My head spun as I tried to analyze my dilemma.

Whatever their motives, I realized they would never allow me to leave the narrow family that Dad headed. It occurred to me he was so out of control he might prefer to lose me to death than to another man. My life was clearly in danger. Serious danger. Whatever analysis I might choose to apply to the situation, a sense of terror overwhelmed me.

CHAPTER SIX

I suffered through the night, thoughts chasing my fears into nightmares. About six o'clock in the morning, I called Sherwin. "We have to get married today, not next week."

He sighed. "Why today, sweetheart? We'll marry as we planned, after the summer school term is over."

"My parents came here last night, dragged me out of bed, and launched into a full-blown rage for over an hour."

"What'd they say?" He sounded as if he struggled to imagine my parents going that far.

"What we've been hearing all along. It's always been absurd, but now they're making more threats. They even brought up their call to the dean of men here and how they asked him to stop our marriage."

"Yes. But remember that he is now a good friend."

"Well, they kept on." I mimicked their voices. "Mother said, 'It will cost your father his reputation. He may not even be able to make a living. We won't put up with it!' Dad said, 'We'll disown you if you marry Sherwin. We will stop financing your education.'"

"They'll get over it. They have Jewish friends, and your dad has Jewish patients."

"I know. I know. But Dad has become angrier by the day since we announced our engagement. Sherwin, they nearly became physically violent with me. It all seems so much worse after last night. If I go with them to the opera on Sunday, I'll be taking the risk that Dad will push me off a cliff in the mountains."

"Oh, Patty, I don't think your father would try to kill you."

"Sherwin, I'm frightened. I am only twenty, so I'm still a minor. He can do anything to me. If he doesn't kill me, he can put me in the psychiatric hospital to prevent our marriage." I took a shaky breath and continued. "He could institutionalize me." During this time period, I knew that women under the age of twenty-one, if not married, were still subject to control by their parents.

After a brief pause, I said, "You're twenty-one, so you're safe. I'm safe only if I am married." I knew I was facing another crossroads moment. "I have two choices. We can marry today, and I will be safe, or I can tell them I have broken up with you. In that case, they'll probably insist I leave the University of Colorado."

He responded without hesitation. "My darling, I love you so much. I've said I would never let you go, and I won't. But we can't get a license in Colorado and be married before Sunday. We don't want to get Fs, so let's leave for Wyoming just as soon as we can both drop out of the university's summer session. It's important enough to forfeit this semester. How soon can you be ready?"

"How about ten o'clock?"

"I'll fill the car with gas."

CHAPTER SEVEN

W e had reached Fort Collins before it occurred to us that Wyoming might have an age limit for marriage. After we found a public phone, we called and received the bad news: both parties must be twenty-one. We would have to drive to New Mexico. We turned around and passed through Boulder, Denver, and Colorado Springs. By four o'clock, we realized we couldn't make it to Raton, New Mexico, before the courthouse closed. Again, we located a public telephone. A kind woman in the clerk's office said she would wait for us.

At seven o'clock, we checked in with the clerk and paid the requested fee. She referred us to a clergyman across the street, and he recruited two witnesses and conducted the ceremony. Our wedding took just a few minutes. At last, I felt safe. I had my life back. But I was not the happy bride I should have been, because I was focused entirely on my safety.

We checked into a nearby motel. As soon as we reached our room, Sherwin said, "I'm so excited. I've wanted you every day since we met. Now I can finally make love to you."

I didn't have any special feeling about the next few minutes, but it pleased me to make Sherwin happy. I was also pleased that we knew enough to protect me from a pregnancy neither of us wanted.

The next morning, we called Sherwin's mother and father. They welcomed me into their family with great delight and asked us to stay with them in their one-bedroom apartment while we decided what came next. Their actions confirmed my initial opinion of them: Sherwin's father was a prince and his mother a lovely, charming, down-to-earth woman.

After we arrived in Denver, Sherwin's parents called mine. Whoever answered said only, "It is a terrible tragedy."

A tragedy? The blunt comment stunned me, but a welcome sense of relief soon erased my shock. Terror had overwhelmed me for weeks, but I finally felt safe. My life was no longer in danger. That realization, combined with the enormity of what had happened, seemed too profound to contemplate. My head wouldn't stop spinning.

Still, we needed to deal with the realities of life. Sherwin's aunt Adeline offered us a rent-free year in her cottage in Hollywood, California. We accepted and drove to Boulder to pack.

Our trip to California gave us the opportunity for a wonderful honeymoon. We drove across the mountains; through the desert; and into sunny, moist California where the beer signs said, "It's LUCKY when you live in California." We agreed. We were indeed lucky to live there. I began to feel our lives would work out.

Shortly after we crossed the state line, I said, "Our job now is to figure out how to get back in school."

Sherwin said, "My darling, we'll both finish our undergraduate degrees and then go to graduate school. I'll enroll in medical school, and if you want a Ph.D., I'll support you. Maybe we'll have to alternate, with one of us in school one year and the other the next."

"Yes, thank you. I surely do appreciate your remembering that our mutual interest in education brought us together."

In Hollywood, Aunt Adeline showed us around the property we would call home for the next year. Her picturesque cottage sat on a two-acre parcel with lush gardens at the back of the property.

We met the rest of the family, including two maiden aunts and some of Sherwin's cousins and their families. They could not have been more welcoming. We expressed our gratitude more than once. Finally, we were safe and connected to a loving family. We looked forward to settling down, re-establishing our schooling, and beginning our new life together.

It was not to be. One evening, a man jumped the fence, ran by our cottage, and dashed out the front of the property. I became terrified once more. Did my parents send the man to harass and frighten us? It wasn't likely since they didn't know where we'd moved.

That night, Sherwin and I agreed to sleep in each other's arms for safety. We had become as close physically as we were emotionally.

We called the police the next morning, and they told us two mobs had made our section of Hollywood a turf for their war. A man was found dead in his car a few days later, which assured us the odd occurrence had nothing to do with us. However, having a turf war in our new, upper-class neighborhood didn't promote a sense of safety.

CHAPTER EIGHT

A few days after we reached Hollywood, Sherwin's parents received a letter from my mother, addressed to me. They forwarded it to California. Her words made it crystal clear we were mistaken in assuming they would change their minds.

> Dear Patsi,
>
> I am enclosing the ticket for the Central City opera last Saturday. The fact that it can be returned to you, unused, tells more about the whole tragic affair than any dozen pages which could be written. For it is a symbol.
>
> First, it represents all of the things which you are giving up: financial security, musical education, ability to attend the kinds of things you have always loved, and unquestioned acceptance by your equals.
>
> Second, it represents the complete lack of personal integrity which has characterized your relations with us during the last few

weeks. We have always trusted you implicitly and relied unquestionably on your sense of fair play. However, in this whole matter, there has been no honesty, no sincerity, no intelligent response—no Patsi as we have known her.

Third, it represents the utter rejection by you of your family and all that it represented. The whole thing was done without regard to the pain which it would cause all of us. You were a member of a family, each of whom loved you greatly and each of us was very proud of you. Each of us is very sad, and our close friends mourn with us the loss of a lovely daughter. You can hardly be happy yourself at the thing you have done. You have killed something for all of us, but you yourself have all the rest of your life to live with this. There is no way that you can ever forget, and no happiness which you can ever obtain can completely compensate for the sorrow upon which your joy is built.

Times may change for you, and the day may come when you are heartily sick of association with one who knows <u>all</u> of the answers <u>all</u> of the time while you are ever-increasingly pushed into a subordinate position. Your own self will cry out to be heard and to be recognized for the person which you were before this tragic thing alienated, changed and completely blinded you. When that time does come, the door will be open for you, but for you <u>alone</u>. If you need help, don't let your false pride keep you forever committed to a mistake. Meanwhile our hearts go out to you who has so much...so terribly much to learn.

Love, Mother

I stared at the letter with astonishment, while my mind reeled with thoughts: *Mother, what are you talking about? "The whole tragic affair" was your idea. You and your friends want to stop mourning? Issue an apology to me and my husband! You don't even need to do that. Just say, "Return, both of you; all is forgiven." It would be easy. You started it. You can reverse it.*

I stood and paced around the room.

You can't be serious when you write that everyone in the family agrees with your anti-Semitism. The grandmothers? Aunt Grace? All the uncles? All my cousins? All my friends?

Come back alone? You must be kidding. I would lose my precious Sherwin. Did you know that toward the end of "this whole thing," I thought my life was in danger? My lifestyle certainly was. What would you do to me if I returned now? You and my father are simply crazy.

I wanted to scream at my mother and shake some sense into her. Nonetheless, her letter forced us to acknowledge that my family was lost to me; they were gone.

I began to experience prolonged emotional streaks during which I sobbed for about half an hour, slept, and then returned to reality. Most of the time, I was able to participate in what otherwise would have been a happy marriage.

I asked myself, *how did I get here? How could this possibly have happened to me?*

I was the daughter of a family that sought, not always successfully, to join the upper class, but their ambitions did not affect me. I had graduated at the top of my high school class and received a scholarship to Mills College. I had headed into a musical career. Now, with my darling husband, we struggled to survive. What happened?

Let me tell you about it.

SECTION 2:

A MOST PECULIAR
UPBRINGING

CHAPTER NINE

When I was born on June 2, 1931, Dad was a young doctor, and my mother was working on her PhD in biochemistry. Although they adored me, I spent my early childhood in a strange place. I became a child in residence at a psychopathic hospital and had, at best, a most peculiar upbringing.

When I turned two weeks old, my parents hired Grace Sweeney Wilkinson, aged sixty, to care for me during the day. She told them she did not want to be called Granny; we were to call her Nanny. The word "nanny" was not in common use as a job title then, but it suited her.

She lived a few blocks away with her husband, a Presbyterian minister, and their fifteen-year-old daughter, Laura. Nanny's husband did not serve a church but sat on several boards and organizations that paid him a stipend. Nanny took the position because the Great Depression was ongoing, and the family's real estate properties no longer produced sufficient income to supplement her husband's earnings. Nanny and her family became only slightly less important to me than my primary family, and I considered Laura my big sister.

My father had graduated from medical school in 1928 and married my mother immediately. They moved to Rochester, New York, where he served his internship and became a psychiatrist, a relatively new medical specialty. He secured a residency at Colorado Psychopathic Hospital and had nearly completed it when I was born.

Located toward the back of Colorado General Hospital, the facility was known affectionately as Psycho by the doctors and nurses who worked there. People in the neighborhood less affectionately referred to it as the nuthouse. A grocery store and drugstore down the street near Colorado Boulevard served the residents of the area. The building next door to the hospital housed the University of Colorado School of Medicine.

When Dad became a staff physician, his compensation included an apartment within the psychopathic hospital. Our apartment sat just behind the reception desk on the first floor, across the hall from the occupational therapy division. It boasted a living room, dining room, kitchen, bathroom, bedroom, and junior bedroom (or alcove). The place came with running water, heat, electricity, and an icebox.

To keep food cool, the iceman delivered an enormous block of ice almost half the size of the icebox once a week. Delivering ice looked like a hard job. Magically, the old ice had always disappeared by the time fresh ice arrived. The small box offered space for milk and enough food for lunch and maybe dinner.

Occasionally, we ate dinner at home, but we usually walked to the hospital dining room about half a block away. The same kitchen provided meals for the cafeteria and for patients, and despite being institutional food, it tasted rather good. When snow or frigid weather kept us indoors, we could take the tunnel, which ran underground from the nuthouse to the dining room. An underground passage from Psycho to the nursing school also existed. Both were lit by bare low-wattage bulbs every twenty feet or so. Huge pipes ran overhead and sometimes made funny noises. Before I was five, I spent hours in the tunnels riding my tricycle or bicycle, running, and roller skating. I wasn't supposed to play there, but I learned when the tunnels would be in use by hospital staff and managed to avoid getting caught too often.

Eating at the staff-only dining room released my parents from time-consuming shopping, cooking, and cleaning up, which meant we could spend mealtimes in stimulating conversation. Sometimes we sat at our own table, but we usually joined other physicians and their families at the doctors' table. Often the doctors talked about their cases, and a frequent topic of discussion was who would or would not undergo "shock treatment." That therapy, common in the 1930s, has been accurately depicted in some movies. The patients' blood-curdling screams in those films led me to assume it was a terrible experience for the recipient.

As the war in Europe approached, more and more conversation about Hitler's aggression, Chamberlain's appeasement, and Japan's assumption of domination over Asia took place at the doctors' table. Hearing the details about those topics made it seem much worse than a scary movie. I couldn't understand how Chamberlain could give away Czechoslovakia. It wasn't his to give away. Nor could I understand how cleaning my plate at meals would help the starving children in China. I wondered if uncivilized barbarian herds were overrunning the entire world. The scariest part was that those barbarian herds had guns, tanks, airplanes, and bombs, and not just horses and bows and arrows.

Occasionally, a Jewish doctor who had escaped from Germany joined us, sometimes accompanied by his family. They said extraordinarily little about what had happened to them there and instead concentrated on improving their English and fitting into their new home.

As more and more countries fell to the Nazis, the grown-ups mused about what would happen next. As early as 1939, the possibility of the United States being invaded and conquered became more and more frightening. I dreamed that the powerful Nazis reached the east coast, took a giant bulldozer, and dumped the entire east coast onto Denver.

My parents and the other doctors assured me an invasion wouldn't be that bad. Nevertheless, I became convinced that what came next for our country would be horrible.

CHAPTER TEN

The setting for our apartment at the psychopathic hospital had little charm. Our living room windows
looked out onto the east court. They probably intended it to be a
garden, but when we lived there, gravel covered the ground. My
parents had a swing set and sandbox installed, and it became
my private play area.

Facing this area on the third floor were rooms for the very
disturbed women. On the second floor were living quarters
for the less disturbed men. At one time, two young men, ages
twelve and fifteen, occupied the men's ward. I enjoyed talking
to them for hours and hours. Although I kept asking them why
they were there, they didn't know. After I begged my father to
let me meet them, he finally agreed, but it was a disappointing
experience. We couldn't relate to each other face-to-face. When
I returned to the sandbox, our relationship returned to what it
had been originally.

Having men incarcerated on the second floor allowed some
to jump out the window and escape. I thought there might have
been fewer escapes if the hospital had housed those patients on
the third floor, since they couldn't jump to the ground without

injuries. Nor did I think the women, had they been on the second floor, would have jumped.

Twice, I saw a man escape as I watched from our dining-room window. Each time, the man banged on the bars around the windows until he managed to separate them. The banging lasted about an hour. Then the man easily opened the window and jumped. Both escapees landed hard, but they picked themselves up, ran across the courtyard, and climbed over the fence.

Neither my father nor mother was home during the escapes. My babysitter tried to get in touch with someone in authority but failed. She had to call the police to get anyone's attention. One man was caught a few blocks away, but I don't know what happened to the other.

In the summer of 1935, my mother and Dad joined a physician's group on a trip to Europe and left me with Nanny. During their absence, I came down with scarlet fever, a serious disease at the time. She and I were quarantined at the Wilkinson's home, which meant nobody could come into or go out of the house except my doctor until I recovered.

Laura was attending the Colorado Women's College in Southeast Denver and stayed with friends during the quarantine. However, she managed to sneak into the bushes to talk to us through the window after dark.

Nanny must have notified my parents about my illness, but they did not interrupt their trip to return to me. Was I, a four-year-old with a serious and perhaps fatal disease, upset that they stayed away? I don't remember. Maybe my child's mind could not make such connections.

I recovered from scarlet fever, but while Nanny quarantined with me and Laura stayed with friends, Mr. Wilkinson died, probably of old age at their home. Nanny was left to deal with the tragedy, and Laura dropped out of college and took a job in the hosiery department at the J.C. Penney department store.

At age five, I started school at Graland Country Day School, about two miles from our apartment. My mother drove me there the first morning and gave me instructions for walking home. I followed her directions and survived.

My parents enrolled me in public school at Steck Elementary at the beginning of the second grade. My new school was located only three blocks from our apartment, which made it easy to walk home each day.

No other children lived at Psycho, and those in the neighborhood laughed at me. "Ha, ha, ha. You live in the nuthouse; we won't play with you." They didn't call *me* a nut, but their meaning was clear. I remember it as a painful experience for a young child.

About the time I started public school, I met Elizabeth, a girl my age. She lived across Eighth Avenue in the medical fraternity house with her parents, who were caretakers for the house. We enjoyed wonderful times together, and I occasionally went to church with her family.

I also met my dear friend Joan Marshall. She lived up the street with her parents, the proprietors of Child Village, an early day-care center. Joan's mother and my mother had known each other when they were growing up. Joan did not participate in the nuthouse teasing and was the first person allowed to visit me at home. We wandered all over the campus together.

In 1937, just before I started the second grade, Nanny left us to join Laura in San Francisco, where she had moved to find a better job.

With Nanny gone, Mother had to hire another childcare provider. She ran an ad in the *Denver Post* and requested a personal interview with candidates on a Sunday morning. There must have been fifty women in the reception room of Colorado Psychopathic Hospital. Mother singled out one woman and invited her back to the apartment. She said, "I am so sorry I did not specify in the ad that I must have a white girl. I would have no problem hiring you, but the hospital won't allow it."

I thought the woman was much more gracious than I would have been under the circumstances. The hospital certainly served African Americans. Why couldn't they employ them too? That was long before the civil rights era.

One day, as I walked along Ninth Avenue, I came across five African American children alone in a car. The oldest appeared to be around twelve, and the youngest perhaps three. "Where is your mother?" I asked the oldest.

"Oh," the children said in chorus, "she's in the hospital having a new baby for us. She'll be back soon."

I didn't know what to say, so I just nodded and walked away.

Over the next few years, our Rymer family grew when my sister Betty arrived on July 20, 1938, followed by my brother John on October 31, 1941, and then my sister Anne in 1944.

Betty and I slept in bunk beds in the bedroom alcove after she graduated from her crib. When Johnny was born, his nursery took over the dining room, which Mother had previously converted to her study. Two adults and three children made the apartment very crowded.

My parents, anticipating the situation, had purchased a lovely colonial home in Crestmoor Park, about a mile and a half from the hospital. They paid $17,000 for the property, and we moved there in June 1942.

We settled into a wonderfully normal life, but the move marked the end of my growing-up years in the nuthouse. I'd grown accustomed to its oddities.

CHAPTER ELEVEN

Beginning at age five, I accompanied my parents on trips around the state when my father testified as an expert witness in a murder trial. One trial involved a particularly grisly murder near Walsenburg, Colorado, in which the victim had been found in his car, shot and stabbed. Everyone in the courtroom, including me, saw the horrible pictures.

My father had examined the accused, the victim's widow, to determine her sanity. He declared the woman sane. When she took the stand, the prosecutor asked if she had killed her husband. He posed the same question many times, and each time she said, "No."

Dad became the darling of prosecutors because he found everyone he examined to be sane. Shortly before his death, I asked him if he considered anybody insane. He said, "Yes, insanity might be drug induced."

My father believed in the death penalty. He said the death penalty was society's way of excising a societal cancer that could cause a lot of damage if left unchecked. "There are just some people who are so awful that, if we want to have a decent society, we don't want them around." When asked if the death penalty were a deterrent to future crimes, he replied, "Nonsense."

As I approached my teenage years, I became more inquisitive and more opinionated. When I was thirteen, my father traveled to Canon City, Colorado, the location of the Colorado State Penitentiary. Most likely, he needed to examine or re-examine someone whose trial and conviction involved an insanity plea. He took Mother and me with him.

The warden invited us to lunch. He looked the part: heavy-set, balding, and gruff, a no-nonsense type who appeared to be a decent man. During the luncheon, he and my father discussed the McNaughton rule as a defense to murder. The rule is applicable (a) if the defendant did not know what he was doing or (b) if he knew what he was doing but did not know it was wrong. Both my father and the warden seemed to think a lot of people in prison didn't belong there, but they did not say why.

The discussion evolved into the difference between right and wrong. Although I understood the business about the defendant not knowing what he was doing, I really didn't get the other part. I chimed in, asking, "What is the difference between right and wrong?" While I certainly agreed one human being killing another was wrong, what if the victim had come at the accused with a knife? Surely defending oneself wasn't wrong. Our great nation had killed hundreds of thousands of Germans and Japanese, but they had murdered our people. We were acting in the self-defense of our nation.

Mother asked if we could be excused and guided me to the restroom. "You will have an opportunity to ask these questions later," she said. "When you go to college, if you want to debate the meaning of words, you can study semantics. If you want to explore the depths of the existence of or the difference between right and wrong, you can become a philosopher. If you want to deal with the mental state of persons accused of murder and the legal standards for evaluating their mental state, you can discuss it endlessly if you become a lawyer."

"That's it; that's it," I said. "I'll be a lawyer. It's better than being a psychiatrist, because lawyers get to walk around the courtroom and ask the questions. The doctor must sit still and answer them. That's boring."

"Well, fine; we will support you in that," replied Mother. "However, right now you are a guest of the warden of the Colorado State Penitentiary, who is entertaining the acting director of the Colorado Psychopathic Hospital and his family, and your questions are inappropriate. If you can't stop asking them, you will have to go sit in the car."

We returned to the table, and I stopped asking questions for a decade or so.

CHAPTER TWELVE

Two places where I could have asked questions without criticism were my grandparents' homes. My parents often left me with each set of grandparents, giving me exposure to two lifestyles vastly different from what I experienced at home.

Grandmother and Grandfather Rymer reminded me of a Grandma Moses painting. They lived in Lakewood, not far from the National Jewish Hospital, on land just short of an acre. Granddad bought a house more than fifty miles away, dismantled it, transported it back to their property, and put it together board by board. Their previous house in Denver lacked plumbing and electricity, while the Lakewood house offered limited electricity but no plumbing. A well stood just outside the door, and their water supply consisted of what they pumped and carried into the house.

A barn near the front door housed a cow, about ten egg-laying chickens, and a rooster. My grandparents sold the eggs and milk, and they leased a wheat field to bring in additional income.

Near Thanksgiving, a turkey would appear. Mother and Dad and I, Uncle Martin and Aunt Grace, my cousin Sally, and Great Aunt Donna would arrive early in the morning. The men captured the turkey, chopped off its head, and let its body run around the yard until it dropped dead. The women plucked the bird's feathers, prepared it for cooking, and roasted it in the wood stove.

An interurban train ran through the property behind the barn twice a day, running from Denver and Golden. It traveled only thirty miles an hour, but that seemed like a rocket to me. Grandmother and Granddad explained property lines, and I never tired of exploring their farm whenever I visited them.

My Rymer grandparents were serious folks but always kind to me. Grandmother was a member of Eastern Star, and both were good, church-going Republicans (the party of Lincoln) who did not try to indoctrinate me with controversial ideas.

Grandmother and Grandfather Reinhardt lived in Boulder, Colorado, now a suburb of Denver. At the time, it was a hard drive an hour away. They lived in the high Colorado Mountains when they first married. In the fall, Granddad would go into Denver to buy huge sacks of flour, sugar, and lard. The family also ate squirrels, rabbits, and whatever else Granddad shot. One year, he bought a gold mine, but after he tried unsuccessfully to recover gold for many years, he discovered it had been salted, which meant the sale was fraudulent. Grandmother then took their four children to Boulder, leaving him a note saying he could find his family there.

As a veteran of the Spanish American War, Granddad received preference for a job as a mailman. They bought a house in Boulder and enjoyed a comfortable life a few blocks from the University of Colorado, where Mother attended and thrived.

Grandmother Reinhardt took religion seriously. She often chatted with me about our Lord, saying, "God made the heavens. He made the stars. He made the sun and the moon."

I repeated this valuable information to Mother and Dad when I was about six, and Dad threw a fit. "Patsi," he said, "Mother and I do not believe in God!" He turned to Mother. "I don't want them talking to her like that. We can't leave her with them unless they can shut up about religion."

"I agree," she replied. "It's close to child abuse."

I didn't get upset, but their reaction puzzled me. Clearly, there were different viewpoints in my family.

During grade school, junior high school, and high school, I made my parents happy by being a "good girl." Dad was difficult to figure out, but I had learned to sidestep him to get what I wanted while keeping the peace.

* * *

In 1951, my efforts to sidestep Dad and keep the peace shattered. Thinking through my early life and my relationship with my parents provided no enlightenment about what had happened to me—and to us.

Nonetheless, Sherwin and I had escaped to Southern California, and life moved forward.

SECTION 3:

THE MAKING OF
A PHYSICIAN

CHAPTER THIRTEEN

S herwin's family had totally accepted me and proved it by often expressing sympathy and love. Their acceptance opened the way for us to discuss our situation with them in detail. They responded with incredulity. "Don't worry, sweetheart, you haven't been disowned; they'll get over it," said one of his aunts. After fearing for my life at the hands of my own parents, such warmth and support brought me great comfort.

Still, Mother's letter was incontrovertible. At least for now, we would need to go ahead with our lives as if I'd been orphaned.

The deadline for fall admissions had passed, so neither of us was accepted at UCLA. We needed to return to college that fall, but it couldn't be at the University of Colorado, where neither of us felt safe. Enrollment for fall admission at the University of Utah had not yet closed, so we headed there.

We moved into a one-room off campus, euphemistically called an apartment, with a bathroom across the hall. Sherwin enrolled in the courses he had promised the medical school he would complete, and I signed up for twenty-two units, primarily in music. We were set on obtaining our degrees there.

Then another defining moment occurred.

Sherwin received a letter from the University of Colorado School of Medicine. Rather than the acceptance we thought was guaranteed, the envelope contained a rejection. The news derailed our plans and left us feeling devastated.

We had little doubt that my parents had engineered the rejection. What they had done to me had been a family issue, which made it my problem. Pressuring the medical school to reject Sherwin could only be viewed as a direct attack on him. I couldn't allow their hostility to harm my husband and his educational aspirations. Did we have an alternative? We certainly did.

Sherwin remained silent for several minutes and then said, "This is a heartbreaking thing." I had not seen him exhibit shock before. He was the calm one in our relationship. But this threw him. He grew pale and began shaking.

"Yes, it is," I said. "But we have options. We'll have to find another school."

Sherwin must have anticipated the possibility of being barred from attending medical school in Colorado, as he had applied to a few other schools. He told me he had been accepted into the school in Geneva, Switzerland, so that was an alternative. We discussed the pros and cons, and I expressed doubts.

"I don't think you can learn French while you are in medical school. We're in too vulnerable a position for you to risk failing in your first year. Besides, if I am going to have to work (which was becoming more and more likely), I cannot find a job in Geneva when I don't speak French."

Sherwin agreed.

It felt good to be taking charge. For the first time in months, I saw a glimmer of hope for our future. I went to the library and collected the names and addresses of every medical school in the world. I typed and re-typed Sherwin's letter of application and mailed them with his transcript to dozens of institutions. We eliminated the Soviet Union, China, and Israel. Israel had been a nation for less than five years, and it seemed too unstable.

An application to Egypt was returned with a letter saying only, "Dear Sir: Your application is rejected." We gave up on the third world.

Gradually, the picture brightened. By January 1952, possibilities in Canada, England, and Australia emerged. The school in Canada was too expensive. England, a few years after World War II, still did not have central heating in homes, so it would be too cold there. Sydney, Australia, wrote that they accepted only residents of New South Wales.

Melbourne, Australia, said yes, but their first year repeated some of the courses he had already taken. Still, we thought they might advance him once he was there, so we started making plans in the direction of Melbourne.

CHAPTER FOURTEEN

After we finished the fall quarter at the University of Utah, we drove to Denver sell our car and to say goodbye to Sherwin's folks. We then flew to San Francisco and boarded the airplane for Sydney. No direct flights to Melbourne existed.

In 1952, it took three days to fly to Australia, including the day lost crossing the International Date Line. We stopped for hours in Honolulu, Canton Island, and the Fiji Islands before we reached Sydney.

An unexpected stroke of good luck occurred during our travels. While we sat in a reception area in Honolulu, we met an older couple. Mr. Waters told us he was the chief operating officer of an international industrial company based in Sydney. He and his wife shuttled back and forth between Honolulu and Sydney so they could gain American citizenship. They explained the details, and we felt encouraged to meet a middle-aged couple who were working so hard for something they wanted, just as we were.

Our search for an acceptable medical school intrigued the couple. "What did Sydney say?" asked Mr. Waters. Sherwin produced the letter from Sydney saying they accepted New South Wales residents only. "Interesting," he said.

Mrs. Waters took over. "Do you like the beach? Warm weather? Interesting people? Culture?"

"Yes, yes, yes, and yes," we said in chorus.

"Good," Mrs. Waters replied. "You won't like Melbourne. The weather and the people are cold. There is no good beach. There is no culture. You just won't like it. But you'll love Sydney."

We listened but remained silent. Living in Sydney sounded magnificent, but we already knew the school there wouldn't accept Sherwin.

"How about this?" Mr. Waters said. "If Melbourne is the school you will eventually attend, why don't you stay at a hotel here in Sydney for a few days? Visit with the director of admissions at the medical school in Sydney and tell him that you received his letter, moved here, and are now a resident of New South Wales. Then ask him to admit you."

We discussed the possibility and felt a bit apprehensive about being at loose ends for another week, but Sherwin did it, and it worked. He was accepted into medical school! Our first triumph together prompted us to shout for joy and celebrate for days.

Mr. and Mrs. Waters helped us find an apartment. Although apartments rented for only a few hundred pounds a month, they were unavailable due to Sydney's strict rent control. The market itself made an adjustment by allowing the landlord to charge a deposit for the key that exceeded months and months of rent. Because we couldn't pay the "key money," we accepted a one-bedroom furnished apartment in Darling Point, a suburb of Sydney near Kings Cross, close to the center of town.

CHAPTER FIFTEEN

My agreement with Sherwin would have to be altered, a fact I reluctantly accepted. To give him the opportunity to finish medical school, I would have to find employment. We had based all our plans on his becoming a doctor. Once he became employed as a physician, I could work toward my professional degree. With a heavy heart, I began to look for a job.

Two standards in the Australian job market differed substantially from employment in America. First, by local custom, married women were not employed outside the home. No such rule existed; it just wasn't done. Second, salaries were partially set by the government and were based on gender. A basic wage for men and a basic wage for women existed side by side. Women's salaries were about twenty-five percent lower.

Secretarial jobs were plentiful, but I neither wanted nor thought I could handle the job of a secretary. Instead, I applied for a position at the blood bank, offering my nearly finished undergraduate degree as a reference. In addition, I knew blood bank language: ABO groupings, the Rh factor, and a few other terms. As the head of a blood bank, Mother had talked incessantly about them.

The Sydney blood bank director appeared impressed with my knowledge of the field. He put me in charge of two other technicians in a small, self-contained laboratory. Due to my perceived seniority, I received the basic wage for men. Of more than one hundred women employed at the blood bank, only three of us were married.

Sherwin and I formed friendships more quickly in Sydney than either of us expected. Early in World War II, shortly after Pearl Harbor, the Japanese fleet had been on its way to invade Australia. The American Navy engaged the Japanese in the Battle of the Coral Sea and won the day, saving Australia. You would have thought we were personally responsible for the victory. Ten years after the event, Australians remained grateful to America and appreciative of us personally. Sherwin's colleagues invited us into their homes, where we met their families and friends. Our newfound popularity astonished us, but we took advantage of the opportunity to make dozens of new friends.

Sherwin found the academic work to be harder in Australia than in the US, where daily quizzes, special projects, and midterm examinations measure the progress of a student throughout the year. In Sydney, students sat for one final examination, a make-or-break test covering all they had learned throughout the year. The approach made students apprehensive. Never could a student ask, "How am I doing?" Professors simply did not know.

I settled into my job, and we enjoyed an active social life, but we never forgot the disaster that loomed if Sherwin failed the examination. Our precarious position became a daily concern.

We breathed more easily after he passed Sydney's second year (part of Colorado Medical School's first year) in December 1952 and received one honor. He passed third year in August of 1953 (the balance of Colorado's first year) with two honors.

While we loved Sydney and the Australians, we wanted to base our careers and our lives in America, so we set plans in motion to return to Colorado. We phoned Daddy (my name for Sherwin's father) and sent him Sherwin's transcript with a description of the curriculum.

Daddy met with the dean of Colorado Medical School, armed with evidence of Sherwin's ability to enter the school's second year. The two men discussed the reason for Sherwin's prior rejection. The dean said there had been too much commotion regarding our marriage, but it had died down.

Good news arrived by way of a telegram offering Sherwin admittance to the medical school in Colorado. I gave notice at the blood bank, and we packed our belongings.

Once we arrived in Denver, we found an apartment near the campus where Sherwin would spend the next three years working toward his MD.

CHAPTER SIXTEEN

S herwin and I approached our return to America with a degree of ambivalence, knowing money would be tight. I found a job at an unrelated hospital a few blocks from Colorado General Hospital and began on-the-job training in the laboratory while doing blood tests for the patients there. I started at a salary of $200 per month. Ninety-five dollars of my monthly earnings went for rent.

Although Sherwin's parents subsidized us, I managed our money carefully, making do with what we had.

Almost immediately, something went wrong, and it had nothing to do with money. On Sherwin's second or third day at the school, my mother, who ran the Belle Bonfils Memorial Blood Bank on campus, pulled Sherwin out of class. She asked him to accompany her to her laboratory, claiming she needed information on blood type for all medical students. She asked him to roll up his sleeve, inserted a needle into his arm, and took a sample of his blood.

When he came home that afternoon, he told me my mother had taken his life's blood. He said the experience had terrified him, and he wondered if she had poisoned him. His reaction reminded me of what I'd felt when my parents asked me to go to the mountains with them.

Assuming she really needed blood types on each student, we both knew she could have asked a technician to obtain a sample from Sherwin. That my mother performed the blood draw herself appeared to be payback. She might as well have said, "Okay, you won this round; you got into medical school. Now I will get even."

Sherwin became preoccupied with the thought that my mother had threatened him personally. Eventually, his fear turned to anger. Sherwin could do nothing to Mother or Dad, so he directed his rage toward me. His comments implied that he blamed me for putting him in a dangerous position with my parents, but we both knew it was my relationship with him that angered them.

The irony was circular, and I had been assigned the role of the underdog. After everything I had done to minimize my parents' ludicrous hostility toward me (because of Sherwin) and what my marriage had cost me, our marriage might be in jeopardy.

The situation prompted the thought of another strange irony. Perhaps Sherwin believed that by marrying me and becoming the son-in-law of an outstanding senior physician, he would elevate his status within the medical community and broader society. When my parents decided I was no longer their daughter after I married Sherwin, he could no longer benefit from the relationship. Perhaps, in his mind, he had no further use for me as his wife. He must have forgotten that the entire situation existed because of him.

Since the beginning of our marriage, I had dealt with my losses by crying, sobbing for half an hour every month or so. Sherwin's hostile behavior added to my losses. He had changed, and so had our marriage. He started a pattern of verbal abuse, picking on some irrelevant matter and beating it into me until I started sobbing again. His complaint would be trivial. After attending a dinner hosted by a colleague, he said, "You poured your own wine last night. Don't ever do that again. I was so embarrassed I couldn't stand it."

When I heard that, my mouth gaped open. I could have responded, "You didn't pour my wine, so I had to do it myself." Or maybe I could have said, "The host didn't pay any attention to me, so I did it myself." But I said nothing because I had become afraid of him.

One day, he said, "You don't know how to dress; you are so unattractive looking." Then he hammered the issue until I again started to cry.

I reminded him we were on a tight budget. Even with the help Sherwin's parents provided, I could barely keep myself dressed in any clothes, much less those suited to a fashion horse. I purchased two medical technologist uniforms for ten dollars each. They lasted the entire three years. Every eight months I paid five dollars for a pair of shoes.

When I told him I'd taken the car in for a lube job and oil change, he browbeat me and claimed he'd lubed the car the week before and paid for it, although there was no evidence he had done so.

My perfect, loving husband had become neither perfect nor loving. The common theme centered around four putdowns: I embarrassed him. I was an inferior being. I wasn't good enough for him. And I was incredibly stupid.

At the end of each instance of abuse, we would not speak for a few days. Then we reconciled with explosive sex. A month later, another verbal barrage would occur.

Our mutual fear of my parents continued. My job required me to occasionally visit the blood bank. I did all I could to avoid going there at all. When my supervisor asked me to join her one day, I told her my nemesis worked there and pleaded with her to excuse me. She graciously did.

In those difficult years, a few happy events occurred. My teenaged sister Betty dropped by our apartment one Saturday afternoon. As a child, she had been gorgeous, and she'd grown more beautiful. We chatted as sisters for several hours, with no mention of the strange situation that existed in our family.

On my twenty-fifth birthday, as Sherwin was about to graduate, I passed by Mother in a crosswalk. She looked directly into my eyes as she said, "Happy birthday." Gone was her prior braggadocio. Gone was the arrogance. She looked as if she realized she had lost something valuable.

I said, "Thank you," and walked on.

As unhappy as our time in Denver had been, our overriding goal was getting Sherwin through medical school. Neither of us wavered from that objective. At some point, a seed of realization sprouted in me that after sacrificing my parents, my family, my education, and my financial security to marry Sherwin, I could lose him too—all due to the fallout from my sacrifice. Still, the goal of acquiring Sherwin's medical degree overrode all else, so I killed that seed of realization before it could grow into reality.

I turned my mind to our future beyond medical school. In the mid-1950s, internships and residencies were assigned by a master system. I had longed to return to San Francisco after spending the summer there with Nanny and Laura when I was nine, followed by a month with them at age fourteen. Nanny and her family were not involved in the break with my parents, and our relationship remained as solid as ever.

Sherwin's maternal family lived in Los Angeles, but northern California enchanted him as much as it did me, so he applied for an internship at the University of California, San Francisco. When they accepted his application for a medical/surgical internship, we were thrilled!

Just before we moved away from Denver, Sherwin's uncle died and left him his car. We traded it for a newer model. In June 1956, we sold our furniture and headed to California, just as we had done five years previously. This time we drove there in a new car. We were heading to San Francisco, and my husband was finally a physician. What we both would have thought impossible five years earlier had become our new reality.

The journey reminded us of our honeymoon trip. We traveled through the mountains and the desert and then crossed into California, our promised land.

CHAPTER SEVENTEEN

San Francisco was as glorious as I remembered. We found a furnished apartment in a private home high above the ocean. Although it was not within walking distance to the hospital, our new home offered a spectacular view that compensated for the inconvenience.

Sherwin told me the director made it clear during their introductory meeting that new interns would work day and night. He'd said, "If you have anything important to do, like having a baby, do it today, because you won't have time once your internship begins."

No matter how many hours Sherwin would be working, I needed to find a job. I began my search right away. I had taken a class in lifesaving and water safety from the Red Cross in Denver. As part of the class, I had written a paper on managing a recreation department in a private club. I stopped by the Women's City Club on Post Street and interviewed with the director. Located in a large building dedicated to widows of World War I, the club featured a swimming pool where their elderly members swam in the morning. Students from local parochial schools used the pool for their physical education classes in the afternoons.

The director, a Mills College graduate, was intrigued by my bid to become what I called the recreation director. I said I would supply lifeguards, which they did not yet have, and organize a structured program for the teenaged girls. She hired me on the spot.

After learning how to teach water ballet, I organized the girls for an aquacade. I directed and produced two presentations to the joy of almost everyone involved. After all the overwhelming problems I had encountered with both my parents and Sherwin, I finally had legitimate reasons to feel proud of myself.

Gone was the overriding fear and antagonism we experienced in Denver. We had escaped the sphere of my parents' direct influence and felt safe for the first time since we married. Sherwin's verbal abuse lessened, as did the sad times when I remembered and relived being violently thrown out of my family.

Only when we attended a big party, which happened frequently, did my newfound happiness waver. Sherwin would disappear as soon as we arrived, and I was left to interact with other hospital house staff and their wives or girlfriends for three to four hours. As a married woman, I couldn't participate as a party girl. I couldn't appear to be looking for another partner. Most people were too polite to inquire about the nature of our relationship, but I knew they noticed when my husband dumped me at the door on entry.

When left on my own at a party, I felt a bit like a gopher must feel when his underground home has been poisoned. I had no place to go. I felt uncomfortable and vulnerable as I watched people interacting around me, but I saw no alternative.

Sherwin and I became friends with an unmarried couple, and the man often treated his girlfriend the same way Sherwin treated me. One evening, my unmarried friend turned to me and said, "I've had enough." I joined the search for her boyfriend Mark, who she found talking with Sherwin. She walked up to them and told Mark what she thought of being left on her own at the party. She said, "I do not know what purpose you had in bringing me here and then abandoning me, but your behavior is unacceptable. I am now leaving the party, and I am leaving your life unless I hear from you tomorrow."

We did not see either member of the couple after that, but Sherwin no longer abandoned me at a party. An uneasy sense of peace settled over me.

We had reached the point where Sherwin's income was sufficient to provide for a family. While he and I pretended we didn't want children while we lived in both Australia and Denver, neither of us was serious about it. I had no intention of leaving the marriage without children, even if our problems returned, as long as no physical violence occurred.

Becoming pregnant changed me. The sadness of losing my family all but disappeared, and I felt less alone. It occurred to me that I would never be isolated again. Our son, Nevin Lane Miller, arrived on February 21, 1958, about a week after I took leave from my job. He weighed nine pounds, one and one-half ounces. During labor, my doctor asked when I had last been swimming. When I said, "Last week," he appeared amused.

I stayed in the hospital for five days, as was customary at the time. Nevin stayed in my room with me, which was a new practice. I learned to nurse him, change him, and play with him. At home, I arranged our small dinette as a nursery. Sherwin seemed happy, saying, "You had a nice baby."

Soon after we brought Nevin home, however, signs of Sherwin's narcissism began to emerge. When my son was about three weeks old, I fed and changed him and put him down for a nap. I went to our bedroom to lie down, as I still felt quite tired from the all-night labor before Nevin's birth.

According to what I'd read, babies often cry just before they fall asleep, and Nevin was crying. Sherwin was not going to put up with it. He came into the bedroom and said, "The baby's crying. You wanted to have a baby, so take care of him."

I so wanted to say, "Sherwin, the baby is your son. He will remember who cared for him and who didn't. If you don't like his crying, why don't you pick him up and soothe him?"

Of course, I didn't say that. I never, ever argued with Sherwin. By the time I reached Nevin, he had fallen asleep, and the subject was dropped.

CHAPTER EIGHTEEN

S herwin's internship ended June 30, 1957, after which he completed one year of internal medicine residency in San Francisco. Then he decided he didn't want to be an internist, but instead take care of ears, noses, and throats and earn much more money, so he chose otolaryngology as his specialty. His preference was to study with a doctor at the University of California (UCLA), so he arranged for a three-year residency there.

Our decision to move to San Francisco from Denver had been mutual. The decision to move to Los Angeles was not. I wanted to remain in San Francisco where I could have returned to my job as recreation director at the Women's City Club. Unfortunately, it didn't pay enough for me to live on my own with my baby, so I had no choice but to move to Los Angeles with Sherwin.

Besides, he still had an obligation to me, and I knew I had to be his wife for him to fulfill it.

We moved into a two-bedroom apartment in west Los Angeles near UCLA that we furnished with new, high-quality items. Despite my issues regarding Sherwin, I had to admit he was a good provider.

One bedroom became Nevin's nursery. I enjoyed staying at home with him and socializing with other mothers. I joined a group of women dubbed the House Staff Wives. We played bridge together and talked about our children. I also became active in the League of Women Voters. Sherwin's extended family in Los Angeles included us in their activities, and our life entered a peaceful, calm, and almost happy period.

I checked into the possibility of attending UCLA, but they were not at all interested in having a married woman as a student. Then I discovered a correspondence division at the University of California at Berkeley. I embarked on a years-long effort to acquire enough credits to return to campus and work toward my degree. My initial desire to pursue a career in music had passed, and I still had not settled on a field that interested me.

Early in 1960, it occurred to me that I might give swimming lessons to women who did not know how to swim but who lived in houses with pools. Many of those women had children who were learning to swim. I negotiated a deal with a swimming pool cleaning service to provide me with their clients' names and addresses. When I sent out a direct mail solicitation about my availability as a private swimming instructor, I became busy instantly.

I charged five dollars per lesson, with a minimum of ten lessons, paid in advance. Initially, I traveled by bus between my clients' homes, but I quickly realized I needed a car to do the work. I purchased a Fiat 500 for $500 and serviced more than twenty clients by the end of the summer. Helping women who felt embarrassed by their inability to swim in their own pools thrilled me.

Sherwin's only comment about my enterprise was that my expenses, including the car and a babysitter, cost as much as I earned. While he was technically correct, he did not take into consideration the happiness my business brought me. I had devoted my summer to helping women. I soon had to stop, however, as I was newly pregnant with Stefani.

I read extensively about early child rearing and became convinced that babies should be on a schedule. Sherwin and I didn't talk about child rearing. We seldom discussed anything substantive. The more he learned in his residency, the more expertise he thought he had about everything and everybody. In her letter to me after he and I married, Mother had mentioned Sherwin's "knowing it all." His attitude proved that she had been right in that respect.

Sherwin generally fell back on the excuse that he was too busy working to spend time with his family. He would arrive home about eight thirty at night and be angry that Nevin was asleep. Sherwin told me he did not believe in schedules for babies and claimed he had come home early to see his son. Their relationship was more important than Nevin's schedule, so I let him wake his son and play with him.

That year, an astonishing event occurred. About ten o'clock one Sunday morning, the doorbell rang. When I opened the door, there stood my mother, obviously distressed. "Can I come in?" she asked. She told me she'd traveled to west Los Angeles to consult with a small hospital in the process of setting up a blood bank.

I said, "Of course." Sherwin was home at the time, and he told her she was welcome. He stayed for about twenty minutes and then left for the hospital. Both her visit and his reaction amazed me.

Mother and I spent the day together. Nevin was a little more than three years old, and Stefani had been born a few months earlier. My mother interacted with both children, reading to Nevin and holding Stefi for long periods of time. She easily stepped into the role of grandmother, and we did not discuss what she had called "this whole thing" ten years before. When the time came for her to leave, I drove her to the airport, where we said a fond goodbye.

Why didn't I reject her at the door? Why didn't I ask for an apology? I wondered about my immediate acceptance of her unexpected visit. Perhaps I didn't have time enough to think through my reaction. But on a subconscious level, I believe I desperately wanted to resolve the ten-year-old estrangement between us.

Several months later, I heard from my aunt that Mother had fallen and was in the hospital. A poorly handled disc surgery had taken its toll on her. Sherwin expressed his objection to reconciliation, and I felt deeply upset not only about the estrangement from my family but about his attitude. I cried often, and my whole body shook for long periods of time. Sherwin's only response was, "Those people hurt you. Why do you want to have anything to do with them?"

Again, he was technically correct. But I needed some type of resolution to move past an aspect of my life that had interfered with my peace of mind for years. I wanted to build a more normal relationship with my elderly parents. Neither Sherwin nor I completely understood the reason for their position about our marriage. On the other hand, when I reread Mother's letter, I realized she had been right in some of her positions. Sherwin hadn't fulfilled his promise as the magnificent man I had believed him to be. In fact, he proved to be the opposite.

I managed to get in touch with Mother and offer support for what turned out to be a lifelong disability. We developed an almost normal mother-daughter relationship after that time. Of course, neither Dad nor Sherwin were in the picture, but I did what I could.

In the meantime, Sherwin did not devote the time he should have to his residency. He found outside work that paid well, and I was grateful for the extra income. Unfortunately, his supervisor at UCLA said he would certify him only if he completed one more year of residency. This time, he wanted to study with a doctor based in San Francisco. I jumped up and down with joy as we planned a return to what we both viewed as our long-term home.

We flew to San Francisco in June 1961 and bought a house on a hill in Marin County, a location we considered the best in the world. Sherwin finished the year of residency and became an otolaryngologist. He opened his practice in a suburb a little north of our house and quickly became successful, as he had been trained to do a unique surgery that used a microscopic technique to reverse hearing loss. No other doctors in the county knew how to do the procedure.

SECTION 4:

A TIME OF TURMOIL

CHAPTER NINETEEN

The sixties were a time of turmoil. Abortion, effective birth control, and the elimination of "fault" divorce became popular subjects of conversation throughout the nation. Civil rights came to the forefront, and the Civil Rights Act passed in 1964 during the Johnson administration. Open opposition to the war in Vietnam emerged, and open marriage became part of the new paradigm of applause for individuality.

My personal life was also in turmoil. We had moved back to the San Francisco Bay Area when Stefani, born February 14, 1961, was four months old. I was breastfeeding her, and I'd been handed responsibility for making our new home into Sherwin's castle. Once, after spending the day gardening, I said, "I hope you don't mind if I concentrate on the landscaping. I'll have to let the housekeeping go for a little while."

He frowned and said, without a touch of humor, "No, I cannot permit that." I gasped, believing we were engaged in a discussion between equals. He seemed to think he was in charge and responded with a directive from the big boss. I remained silent.

Sherwin, like all medical residents, spent many overnight rotations at the hospital when he was on call. Their schedule apparently left them with nothing to do but have affairs with nurses. Sherwin was no exception. I assumed he had flings with many of them during his residencies, but it became clear that his affair with a nurse named Patty was more serious. We discussed their relationship at length. He told Patty he couldn't marry her; then he invited her to our home so she could see why. Patty gave Stefani a bath and joined us for dinner. I never saw her again.

When I was alone, my entire body shook with grief and anger. Although I knew the marriage was almost over, I still had not settled on a profession. I certainly would not leave my husband before I discovered the right career. I also felt it would be easier for our children if I delayed the inevitable divorce until they were older. So, I gritted my teeth and tolerated his adultery.

Our second son, Trevis Kent, arrived on August 7, 1962. Becoming pregnant with him surprised me, but I welcomed his birth. Nevin was then four and one-half years old. Trevis and Stefani were seventeen months apart, and they bonded deeply.

A positive defining moment occurred shortly after Trevis's birth. Long before Nevin could talk, I taught him the alphabet. By age two, he could run his fingers over lettering on public buildings and tell me each letter. A friend with a daughter Nevin's age joined with me in using the Montessori educational method to teach our children. Both were ready to read by age four.

In California, a child had to be four years, nine months old by September 1 of the new school year to attend public school. Nevin was three months shy of the age limit that year. Because he couldn't qualify for public school, I enrolled him in a private school. The law also stated that a child must be five years, nine months old to enter the first grade. After two years in a private school, any child who had completed first grade could enroll in the second grade in a public school. That was our plan.

During the regular session of the California Legislature in the spring of 1962, a bill passed that allowed a child who was lawfully enrolled in kindergarten to advance to first grade under circumstances to be determined by the Board of Education. I wired the governor, Pat Brown, and requested that he sign the bill, which he did. I worked out a set of criteria for the child's advancement to first grade. I proposed that any child who was ready to read should be allowed to enter the first grade.

The school Nevin attended used "The Reading Readiness Test." Any child who scored a nine on the test and completed one year of socialization was considered ready for the first grade. I researched as many pre-kindergarten schools as possible and organized my findings to present to the Board of Education.

The issue of the qualifications for advancement to the next grade was scheduled to go before the board in early September. I appeared at the designated time and waited nearly an hour to make my presentation. A motion was made to allow a child to advance to the next grade if the student had an IQ in the top two percent of the population (140 and up). Before the vote, they allowed me to speak. When I finished, the motion was amended and passed. The IQ level was reduced to the top five percent of the population (125 and above). I felt ecstatic!

I had done what lawyers do. I made a request to a government body and then gathered and presented evidence to support the request. I'd done it all by myself, without coaching or instruction, and I achieved modest success!

At the age of fourteen, I had told my mother I would become a lawyer. That evening, I realized I had been right. I knew that the law would be my profession.

It was clearly a defining moment. Adding to the significance of the moment was having a reporter from the Chronicle take my picture and publish a story about me.

I followed the new educational procedures with Nevin, including enrolling him in public school kindergarten and waiting for the teacher to decide when he qualified to enter the first grade. After he performed well on the required tests, she advanced him to first grade, where he did outstanding work.

CHAPTER TWENTY

After my success with the Board of Education in September 1962, I settled down to a life as a suburban doctor's wife. Sherwin stayed busy with his medical practice, and our three little children took up most of my time. Although I had little time to spare, I spent some of it fulfilling my obligation to participate in the Marin County Medical Association for wives.

Sherwin bought a sailboat, and we entertained general practitioners and internists, spending many weekends on San Francisco Bay. The doctors became better acquainted, and Sherwin's practice grew rapidly.

I devoted the balance of my free time to completing as many correspondence courses as possible. I applied to San Francisco State University, and they accepted me as a student, along with all my music credits and correspondence units. To obtain my BA with a major in history, I had only a few courses to complete, which I could do in little more than one academic year.

While I worked toward my goal of earning a Bachelor of Arts by the end of August 1964, Sherwin embarked on a new social activity. The mid-1960s introduced the concept of an open marriage, meaning both parties could (theoretically) live their own lives without interference from traditional mores and morals, while the marriage continued uninterrupted. Switching partners (also known as "swinging") became an accepted part of open marriage. Books had been written on the subject, and the topic intrigued Sherwin.

Early in 1964, Sherwin performed his magic operation on a young married woman with two children. After she recovered from the successful procedure, my husband invited his patient, Jeanne Mulberg, and her husband, Joe, to our home for dinner. The two families, including our five children, became steadies. We spent days at the beach and enjoyed other family activities as a group. The Mulbergs often stayed at our house until early the following morning. The children enjoyed each other's company, and everything appeared to be perfect, at least on the surface. I suspected Sherwin had started an affair with Jeanne, but I could do little about it.

We decided to drive to Mexico together, one family in each car. After a pleasant day there, we stopped overnight in central California. Joe and I put our children to bed following dinner, and he stayed with his. I went back to the dinner table. I'd had one drink with my meal, and ordered another.

Sherwin and Jeanne were dancing, and I waited for them to return to the table. They saw me but remained where they were, dancing closer and closer. They looked very much like two people who were ready to jump into bed together. It was one thing to know my husband was having an affair and quite another thing to watch it in progress. I had no doubt the dancing would continue to its logical conclusion.

I went back to my room and sobbed until my head throbbed. I longed to get into the car with the children and leave. I couldn't do that. Given the alcohol in my system and my shaky emotional state, we could all be killed on the highway.

Eventually I sank into a troubled sleep. I didn't wake when Sherwin returned to our room.

CHAPTER TWENTY-ONE

M any things cleared in my mind that night, and I experienced another defining moment.

The emotional centrifuge I'd lived in for thirteen years began to transform into a giant whirlpool. Round and round it went, faster and faster. With each significant event, from my parents to my husband, pieces of me had shattered off and spun into the pool. My mother's appearance at my door and the day we spent together simply slowed the process. The shattered pieces and what was left of my core swirled toward the center of the whirlpool and threatened to slip down the drain.

No, that's not right. It is something else.

I had not invited the calumny that had been heaped upon me. What had happened felt more like being trapped in a boxing ring where I had never been evenly matched. I still hadn't grasped my parents' ostensible anti-Semitism, but their behavior had landed a massive punch that almost knocked me out.

Then Sherwin took all I had given him, twisted it around, and threw it back in my face. Every time I had taken a hit, I rose and continued fighting. Watching Sherwin and Jeanne was nearly, but not quite, another knock-out punch. I did get back up.

Still, I was obviously losing. I'd recovered a little from time to time, once when I scored a win at the Board of Education and again when I started back to school. Nevertheless, I couldn't withstand another vicious punch. The next blow would likely be the end for me.

I had one alternative only: I had to escape the boxing ring. If I acted precipitously, however, I'd lose everything. I absolutely had to find a way to leave my situation without sacrificing anything of value that remained.

So, what did I have in my favor that could help me escape the ring? Intelligence? Although I didn't operate at the genius level, as did Sherwin and Nevin, but my native intelligence sufficed. Good looking? I wasn't Miss America or even close, and I bore the scars of childbirth. But maybe I might still attract the kind of man I desired—one who would want for me the same thing I wanted for myself.

Was I being arrogant? Perhaps. But I could go nowhere without self-confidence. Having passed the age of thirty could pose a problem for me, but it was not one I couldn't overcome. I just needed to get started as soon as possible.

The next morning, Sherwin behaved as if everything was normal. We drove home with the children, and life resumed. He returned to his medical practice. I went back to my next-to-the-last semester at San Francisco State. I realized I had already begun to escape the ring.

However, a practical problem emerged. Although I would soon complete my BA, the degree wouldn't allow me to be self-supporting, let alone able to support my children. Both might become necessary in the future. To attend and complete law school, I needed financial stability, which meant staying in the marriage. How would I do that?

The murky details of a plan formed. I knew I would need to make it worthwhile for Sherwin to remain in the marriage. I would have to go along with some of his peculiar ideas.

A week or so after the trip to Mexico, Sherwin asked me to swing with the Mulbergs. He begged and pleaded with me to engage in a sexual relationship with Joe. Joe had repeatedly propositioned me, and I had refused every time. The pain from witnessing Sherwin's adultery with Jeanne had not subsided, and I had no interest in her husband. He did not appeal to me in the least. However, as part of my plan to keep Sherwin in our marriage, I agreed to sleep with Joe.

I saw no legal problems in going along with Sherwin's plan, and he certainly did not point any out to me.

The hour I spent in a motel room with Jeanne's husband confirmed my dislike of him, but it also allowed me to make him into an ally. I wanted to eject them from our lives, and Joe could help me do so. I suspected he had no idea his wife and my husband had been intimate for weeks. When I asked if he knew about Jeanne and Sherwin, he said, "That's not true."

"Joe," I said, "how can you be so blind? Your wife has become my husband's mistress. It is so obvious."

He glared at me for a few minutes and then took me home, with barely a nod to acknowledge my presence.

A few days later, he took his outrage to the next step. He called Sherwin, and they agreed to meet at a local restaurant.

I heard only Sherwin's side of the story, but apparently Joe flipped over a table and started a physical altercation. Someone called the police.

I could imagine the headline in the local paper: *Prominent Kentfield physician in a fistfight with the husband of his mistress.*

No such headline appeared. Nothing happened except that the Mulbergs separated.

CHAPTER TWENTY-TWO

My shattered pieces consolidated and then transformed into a shooting star that forever (well, almost forever) rose upward. I thought Sherwin's affair with Jeanne represented the most defining moment of my life, but there were to be more.

School went well for me after the fight between Sherwin and Joe, and I lost track of what happened with the Mulbergs. At the end of spring semester at San Francisco State College, I needed nine units to complete my undergraduate degree. As a history major, my last class involved a mandatory personal history. The professor referred us to academic sources, and our job was to apply academic history to our family history. My relationship with my mother had reached a nearly complete reconciliation, and she provided the necessary genealogy. My ancestry traced back to before the Revolutionary War on my father's side and to the mid-1850s in Mother's lineage.

As the summer session proceeded, my self-esteem continued to grow. Fourteen years had elapsed since the start of what Mother had called "this whole thing." With few exceptions, those years had felt miserable. I wondered if every woman experienced a similar problem. I doubted that was the case, as my family story strained credulity, and no woman at the time dared to set her own career aspirations at the same level as that of her husband.

One day, I noticed a posting on a bulletin board at San Francisco State offering a roundtrip to Europe for $125 for any students graduating at the end of the summer. "Wouldn't it be wonderful if we took that trip together?" I asked Sherwin.

"I would love to," he replied.

Immediately, I hired a woman who seemed mature and responsible enough to care for the children while we were gone. I paid for the trip and began training Miss Genevieve to care for them. Her bright and sparkling personality meshed with our family and put us at ease, and everyone got along well.

During the first week in August, Sherwin's yes became a no. He claimed he couldn't leave his medical practice because we couldn't afford the loss of income his absence would create. Despite his personal character flaws, Sherwin conducted our financial matters with responsibility and competence.

I left for Europe by myself in early September, feeling confident Sherwin and Miss Genevieve would work together well.

Landing in Paris thrilled me beyond belief. After taking a bus to a hotel on the West Bank, where I checked into my sixth-floor walk-up, my long-awaited vacation began.

I visited many art museums, including the Louvre and the Impressionist Museum. A man I met in the Louvre went out of his way to help me find the reproductions I sought. In our three days together, we went sightseeing in Paris but spent happy hours in his college dorm as well. I found the practices observed by college dorms in Paris strange. Women could visit the men's dorms at any time except between eleven o'clock at night and eight o'clock the next morning. We accommodated the rule by making sure I arrived before 10:30 p.m. and left after 8:15 a.m.

Did I feel sad or guilty that I was now the one having extramarital affairs? Remembering Sherwin's escapades, I enjoyed myself even more.

Next, I traveled through the Scandinavian countries: Denmark, Norway, and Sweden. The women were gorgeous, the men spectacular. Adults tended to speak English, so interaction with people was a pleasant experience. Scandinavia produced beautiful sterling silver and ceramic jewelry, and I collected samples wherever I went.

I had called Sherwin a few times, and he reported that all was well. When I called from Switzerland, I learned much had changed. He said, "I have bad news."

I had been flying high, but I began to plummet to the earth before I even heard the bad news.

He continued. "I had to fire Miss Genevieve. She was drunk all the time."

I hit the ground. Being a drunk explained why a taxi often delivered something to her late at night. I don't know why I hadn't recognized the problem before I left.

I sighed. Then I started to pick myself up. "Do you want me to come home?"

"No. I've hired a college student, and we are doing okay. Come back after Thanksgiving, as you planned."

"I'll try to speed up the trip."

"Fine, but don't change very much. You've wanted this trip for a long time."

I changed my itinerary so that my next destination was Rome. There, I reserved a spot in four tours that appeared exciting. I soon met Jack Johnson, a twenty-six-year-old man who had also just finished his BA, majoring in Greek. Jack and I and several other Americans enjoyed touring, and we bonded as a group.

At the end of each tour, we rode local Italian buses back to our hotels, and we engendered a surprising degree of hostility from the residents. I could never decide whether the Italians were hostile because we were Americans who talked too loudly or because our group included women who were out late at night. Whatever the reason, we were not popular.

Jack and I discussed our travel plans. When I told him I was on my way to Geneva, he modified his itinerary so we could meet in Geneva and then travel to Spain, Portugal, France, and back to England together. By then, it was late October, and most American tourists had returned home.

Jack was gay, and possessed all the characteristics I enjoyed in men, but sex was no part in our relationship. We simply enjoyed our time as travel buddies. I had always liked gay men.

We stopped in Limoges in central France, arriving at our destination late at night. When we asked for two single rooms (*deux chambres seul*), the French laughed, but it worked for us. During the day, we toured the famous china and crystal factory.

We managed two more weeks in Paris and moved on to London. Friends had told us that we could attend almost ten plays in a week in London, and we did. We saw shows on evenings Tuesday through Saturday, matinees Wednesdays and Saturdays, and an interim play between the matinee and the evening performance twice a week. Theaters stayed dark on Sundays and Mondays.

In November, the time came to return to the United States. Jack and I bid goodbye, with no plans to meet again. Our time together and my experiences with other men in Europe had been delightful. In fact, I had felt happier during my travels in Europe than at any other time in my life.

CHAPTER TWENTY-THREE

Sherwin came to the airport to welcome me when I returned from Europe, and he revealed the first bombshell. After talking about the movie *Doctor Zhivago* (adapted from the novel), he told me how he envied the protagonist. "It would be fantastic to have two wives," he said.

I reminded myself that if I were to attend and finish law school, I would have to make it worth Sherwin's while for him to remain in the marriage. Maybe his comment was a hint about what he wanted in our relationship. I made a discrete inquiry as to whether he would truly like to have two wives. He responded obliquely but in such a positive tone that I knew I had an answer I could use to my advantage.

The second bombshell came as a tremendous shock. He would often tell me something he knew I would not like hearing and then try to soften it by saying, "I hadn't planned on it." For example, I would ask, "Are you coming home tonight?"

He would say, "Yes, but later." When he did not return until the next day, his comment would be, "I hadn't planned on it, but ..."

That day, Sherwin's behavior was typical. After stuttering and stumbling for several minutes, he said, "There is something else I need to discuss with you."

"Yes?" I shifted my position to give my order to the waiter, thinking, *I should have expected something would go wrong at home while I was in Europe.*

We finished ordering, and I listened to Sherwin with interest.

"When you left," he said, "we thought Joe's and Jeanne's divorce would not affect us, but it turns out we are involved. I couldn't keep us out of it. As a defense motion, if I am charged with adultery, you probably will be too."

My thoughts tumbled over each other. *Can I never get rid of this liar and his mistresses? So that's the reason Sherwin was so eager to get me into bed with Joe. He knew he was setting me up in a position to be charged with adultery alongside him if Jeanne and Joe divorced. Then I would get nothing, and our agreement regarding school would be gone too.*

The semi-triumphant glow from my European trip darkened and then disappeared as Sherwin talked. I had been outsmarted and outmaneuvered to my great disadvantage. I told him putting me in bed with Joe had been mean and dirty.

He shrugged. "I hadn't planned on it."

Within a week, Sherwin and Jeanne found a lawyer for me. When I met with him, he said, "Yes, you can be charged with adultery and be in a worse position than Sherwin." Women committing adultery were considered less acceptable than men cheating on their wives, at least until the 1970s.

"Even if I did it at Sherwin's vehement insistence?" I asked the lawyer.

"Oh," he said, "that will make it even worse. Your husband will never tell the truth, and you will get nothing. You will be viewed as a loose woman, and you may even lose custody of your children."

I couldn't begin to absorb what he had told me. I held back my emotions until I returned home, and then I cried for hours.

Negotiations continued through the spring of 1965. Eventually, the case was settled—to my disadvantage.

"What about the rest of this lawsuit? What about community property and the house?" I asked. My attorney explained the details. He told me Jeanne and Joe would be ordered to sell their house, but I might not be put in that position if Sherwin had enough money and wanted to continue to carry our house, which he apparently did. It turned out Joe had been able to move the players around the board while paying no alimony and little child support.

Sherwin was clearly unhappy with the settlement of the Mulbergs' divorce. He said we would have to help take care of Jeanne and her children. His use of "we" was telling, but I thought it might fit into my plans.

Sherwin and Jeanne decided to open a dress store in a new shopping center. She would run the store, and they expected it to produce enough money to take care of her. If it did not, he would apparently make up the difference. That really meant *I* would be making up the difference, as any monetary gain for Jeanne represented a loss for me.

Ironically, I could buy dresses for myself at their cost with funds from our community property. I reminded myself that my primary goal was to make it worthwhile for Sherwin to stay in our marriage. Once again, I agreed to something no one else would think of doing.

Later, I brought out the samples of jewelry I had collected from all over Europe. When I showed them to him, he suggested we open a store in the same shopping center as Jeanne's. I reminded him about my plan to attend law school, and Sherwin assured me I could do both. We would hire employees to do the work in the store.

The first store we opened proved to be too small, too far from the most popular part of the shopping center, and too unconventional. The venture did not do well. A larger space became available, and we moved into it. I knew I must make a go of it, but I surprised myself by actually wanting to open a store. We named the shop de Beau's Internationale.

We ordered display cases for traditional merchandise like wedding sets, sterling silver sets, and other bridal jewelry. Purchasing jewelry cleaning equipment and hiring a jewelry salesman well-known in the community came next. The manager I hired became "Mr. de Beau," and he was not only popular but well-liked. When the store grew, I employed a good saleswoman to assist me. She proved capable and did many tasks an owner would otherwise do.

By early 1965, I had felt the need to finally tackle the problem of law school. I would have to work at de Beau's every minute during the fall and Christmas seasons. It would be impossible to attend law school full time while working long hours at the store, let alone spend meaningful time with my children.

After researching my options, I interviewed with two law school deans in the San Francisco Bay Area and asked permission to take a reduced academic load during the fall semester. Dean Gorfinkle at Golden Gate University said he would accept two classes, one procedural and one substantive. I accepted his offer to enter a four-year program (law schools usually complete their total course in three years). I would take only two classes in the fall and make up whatever course I had missed in the summer. Dean Gorfinkle, a charming man, seemed to like both me and my academic record, and he welcomed me with open arms.

Sherwin and Jeanne continued their relationship, and I lived with Sherwin and the children in Tiburon while I started law school in the fall of 1966. Having two "wives" made Sherwin happy, and I began to realize that the bright and fulfilling future I had always envisioned for myself could soon be a reality.

I had enrolled in a course at the Gemological Institute of America, an international educational body in Los Angeles, and acquired a solid foundation in gems and gemology. The curriculum consisted of extensive correspondence courses and four week-long study sessions in Los Angeles. My degree as GG, Graduate Gemologist, Gemological Institute of America was granted on September 2, 1967.

CHAPTER TWENTY-FOUR

When I began my law studies, I attended Golden Gate Law School. By the time I graduated, the name had changed to Golden Gate University School of Law.

I attended class for the substantive course, Torts (the essence of civil law), every Tuesday from 7:00 p.m. to 9:30 p.m. On Thursday evenings during the same time frame, I attended class for the procedural course (how the law works). I had hired full-time, live-in childcare for my children and full-time staff for the jewelry store on Tuesdays and Thursdays.

On the days I attended class, I saw the children off to school in the morning, picked up jewelry left for repair at the store, and then drove to San Francisco to hand off the merchandise to the bench jewelers who did our repair work. From there, I went to Golden Gate, where I studied until my class began.

On my first night, about sixty men and four other women attended class. Joan approached me first, and we became close friends who studied together as often as possible. From time to time, other classmates joined our small study group.

I found the case method for teaching law quite strange. Each case was based on a decision from an appellate court within a complicated hierarchical system. That system started at a local trial court and moved through a long series of higher courts up to the United States Supreme Court. A major issue in every case centered around whether the specific court had jurisdiction, defined as the power or authority to hear the case.

In the late 1960s, the other students (mostly male) and the professors (all male, except for one woman hired in my third year) appeared somewhat uncomfortable having women in the class. The onslaught of female law students did not occur until the mid-seventies.

In the 1960s, law school resembled a training ground for bullfighting. The attitudes of the men varied from outright hostility to a false obsequiousness. One pattern rarely varied. Professors always called upon a woman to recite the details of rape cases, often in all their gory detail.

Despite the male dominance in law school, I formed many friendships, including a "special" friend with benefits each year. During my first year, I started having coffee on Tuesday and Thursday afternoons with a tall and somewhat heavyset man named Rob. A second-year student, Rob carefully explained whatever points of law I did not immediately understand. We soon moved from the coffee shop to the bedroom. Eventually, he told me if his wife were to become aware of our relationship, she would leave him and take everything they owned. I knew divorce had long been based on fault, and adultery was a common fault. We bid our intimacy farewell but remained good friends.

Jimmy G took Rob's place. Jimmy did not have a wife, and his apartment was on my way home, which made it convenient to stop by after class. JG, as I called him, lacked emotional stability but was a decent law student. At the end of our year together, he announced, "You have so much money that you could support me."

The idea of using community property to finance an extramarital relationship irritated me. My attitude may have stemmed from Sherwin's financing of Jeanne's store. It had been purchased and supported with our community funds. I considered it a travesty, and I would not be the guilty party in any such scheme. So that was the end of JG.

By my third year in law school, Gerald became my special friend. I adored Gerald, but he was married, so we too parted company after several months.

In December 1967, Sherwin called out to me from the bedroom next to mine. He was having chest pains, so I drove him to the hospital. It turned out that Sherwin, at the age of thirty-seven, was having a heart attack, a "myocardial infarction," as the doctors called it.

The next day, when I visited Sherwin, his doctor came into the room and asked to see me in the hall. He said, "A woman named Jeanne was here almost all day, sitting on the bed, crying and crying." The physician kept repeating himself. He clearly was angry with me or Sherwin or Jeanne or all three of us, but he had chosen me as the target for his outrage. After a few minutes, I became equally angry with him. How was any of it his business?

I went into my silent response mode and simply stared at him, saying nothing. He continued to harangue me until he ended with, "Well, we know just what's going on. We know what's going on here."

Why was he angry with me? Did he believe it was my fault that my husband was having an affair? Whatever he believed, none of us wanted our private lives to become fodder for gossip throughout the medical community and perhaps the entire county. Finally, I said, "Thank you," and I bid him goodbye.

The doctor continued to care for Sherwin, and we had no additional conversations about our private lives.

I expressed my sympathy to Sherwin for his unexpected health issues. After a pleasant conversation, he said, "Now there must be some sacrifices."

"Yes," I said, "I have been sacrificing for you for decades, for sixteen and one-half years, as a matter of fact." He started to interrupt, but I waved him away.

"It is your turn. If you think this event will prompt me to drop out of law school, please rearrange your thinking. You still owe me your part of our agreement that we would each stay in school until we earned our degrees. You've earned your degree. It is now absolutely your turn to make sacrifices to allow me to earn *my* degree. I have done enough. Enough!"

He said nothing, but he understood everything.

SECTION 5:

A LAWYER AT LAST

CHAPTER TWENTY-FIVE

S herwin came home after his discharge from the hospital and rested for a short time. After he decided to drop out of his medical practice, we canceled the lease on his office space, and he looked into a way to continue paying our bills. My work at the jewelry store continued, as did Jeanne's in the dress shop. We had enough money, at least until I could earn my law degree and find a job.

I had nearly finished law school. I knew I could complete my work in a year if I took extra classes. If I wanted to spend more time with my children, however, it would take two years. I made the decision to slow my progress, but I couldn't stop crying. That told me I'd made the wrong decision, so I reversed course.

I moved into a bed-and-breakfast room with a small kitchenette in San Francisco. Sherwin and I worked out an updated agreement that spelled out his performance regarding our mutual schooling.

I had put up with many of his shenanigans to reach that point, but it had been worthwhile. Neither of us wanted to disrupt the children's lives, so they stayed with him, and I had extended visitation.

We participated in a moot court argument in one of my law classes the day after I moved. JG and I were professor-appointed participants. I wore my wedding rings to discourage him from wanting to resume our relationship. It worked, and I forgot to take them off.

At breakfast the next morning, I sat beside a man who had just moved into a room in the bed-and-breakfast. He introduced himself as Floyd Jones. He appeared to be about my age or a little older. Floyd was not too tall and had curly brown hair and a face that showed he had lived much of his life outdoors. He said he had received a promotion from his company in Kansas City to the executive office in San Francisco. The man had a commanding presence.

After he glanced at my rings, he immediately shifted his attention to another woman at the table. I took the rings off. When he noticed that I'd removed my wedding rings, his attitude changed. We quickly became inseparable.

I wondered if he might, perhaps, be what I was seeking. I had longed for a man who wanted for me what I wanted for myself. Wives at the time were all but required to mimic their husband's desires. For a woman to insist that her husband share her desire to have/do what she wants was unheard of. I let myself think that Floyd might support me on my way up the ladder to becoming a lawyer. And maybe beyond.

Every day during my last year of law school, he and I walked from our lodgings to Market Street, where his office and my school were located. He encouraged me to complete law school and either find a job or open my own office. I imagined our future together with joy. Fortunately, I did not have to worry about whether Floyd and my children would be compatible. He had no children of his own, and he, Nevin, Stefani, and Trevis loved each other.

I finished law school, followed by weeks of studying and sitting for the California Bar Examination. I flew to Colorado and passed their bar examination in April. I could have moved to Colorado to practice law, but I certainly did not want to do that. Instead, I waited another two months to hear from California.

On June 2, 1971, my fortieth birthday, I received a letter notifying me that I had cleared the hurdle. I had passed the exam and would be sworn into the California bar later in the month.

The heavens exploded with brilliant colors in celebration of my triumph.

The boxing ring disappeared.

I had prevailed over all the challenges and obstacles that life had thrown in my path. For the first time in my life, I was in charge of my own destiny. I couldn't have been more excited, thrilled, or triumphant.

I WAS A LAWYER!

CHAPTER TWENTY-SIX

It made logical sense to start my own practice as soon as I could. I had searched for a job between the time I passed the Colorado bar and the bar in California. I qualified only for federal positions, and my prospects for a well-paid position looked dismal. I had no intention of leaving either Floyd or my children, and I had already put Colorado behind me. Besides, the children were well settled with their father, and I did not want to disrupt their lives. Remaining in San Francisco seemed to be the best choice for all of us.

I started my practice one year after the Family Law Act became law. My friend Joan had invited me to open shop in her office in San Carlos. Her offer appeared attractive on the surface, but one drawback concerned me. The space included an exceptionally large room at the front with a smaller office in the back. The only restroom had to be entered from Joan's office, which meant it became unavailable whenever she was at work. On Joan's busy days, my clients and I had to sprint to the local gas station more than a block away if we needed to use a restroom. With reservations, I accepted her offer.

We created an office for me by sectioning off a portion of the large front room with two pieces of sheetrock. Joan and I began to disagree on several issues, and it became clear the close friendship we'd formed during law school had waned.

After Joan and I agreed I should move out, I called Leo, the former assistant dean from Golden Gate University School of Law. He had gone into private practice after leaving Golden Gate, so I called and told him I was looking for a space to rent. He had extra room in his office, so I joined him in Foster City, where he lived and where I already had an apartment. Leo and I were both independent contractors at the time. Later, we asked another attorney in Foster City to join us, and the three of us formed a corporation to practice law as a group entity.

My first case came to me through a lawyer's referral. After enactment of the Family Law Act, the term *defendant* changed to *respondent*. Bill, the respondent in the case, had become involved in a custody battle for his son. His wife claimed Bill was not the father of the little boy, who had been born during their marriage. Blood tests for paternity at that time relied on the ABO system, a method I had worked with in Australia.

Rarely was a man excluded from paternity. After Bill and the wife's paramour took the test, the results revealed a surprise. The "other man" was excluded from paternity. Bill and I met the outcome with great joy. Bill's case became my first win, and he taught me that women do not have a monopoly on misery.

My next client, Lois, arrived at my office the day before her trial was scheduled to begin. A trial is a significant event under any circumstances and an especially big deal in the judicial system. Yet Lois's attorney had apparently made no effort to prepare. Lois showed up at his office without an appointment and heard him say to his secretary, "What does that bitch want?"

I appeared with Lois the next day in court. The judge granted my motion to "substitute in," the procedure for replacing the original attorney. After a few weeks, her husband's attorney and I were able to reach a fair agreement. We couldn't have done so without the well-grounded knowledge of the assets and liabilities we had developed.

Margery, another client, had owned her house before she married. It therefore remained her separate property, but her husband, Hank, demanded what he called "his share." He asked to speak directly to the judge before the case started. His request was rare, but the judge granted it.

Hank, his attorney, Margery, and I squeezed into the judge's chambers, his private quarters. The judge growled something that we considered a go-ahead sign.

Hank said, "Margery and I loved each other; therefore, I think I should have half the house."

The judge frowned. "She had the house before the marriage, and you want half of it now?"

One guideline stressed in law school is that attorneys must inform their clients not to make statements that might go against their interests. Hank's statement did not help his case, and the judge's comment offered a hint about how he would rule.

We proceeded with the trial, and the judge ruled that the house would remain Margery's separate property. He did, however, require her to repay Hank one-half of the taxes paid with community funds. It was the correct ruling.

After I had been in practice a few years, several things became obvious to me. Childbearing and, therefore, alimony and divorce had been revolutionized. Before the Industrial Revolution in America around 1820, women had been so dominated by repeated pregnancies and the raising of their children that they never stopped to think about the proper roles for women or men. That concept began to slip by the 1880s, when the diaphragm was developed in Europe. It would be years before it became available in California.

Access to birth control continued to be limited in the United States until Margaret Sanger began her crusade to give women a degree of freedom from interminable pregnancies. Her efforts resulted in some success, but it was not until use of "the pill" was legalized in 1965 that women could reliably control the reproductive aspects of their lives. *Roe v. Wade,* providing for abortion at will, represented a triumph. Joan, my law-school friend, was the principal author of an *amicus curiae* brief to *Roe v. Wade* at the Supreme Court.

Divorce and alimony, which were closely related, saw many changes as well. Turmoil arose during the sixties, with race relations, military service, divorce, and alimony raising controversy. No one seemed to have any idea what to do about the area of family law. Governor Pat Brown appointed a Commission on the Family, chaired by Professor Herma Hill Kay from Boalt Hall Law School. The Commission proposed one seemingly brilliant idea: get rid of "fault." It became the driving concept behind the Family Law Act.

Men did not seem to understand the bargain that women and men make when they marry. At one time, women married under the premise that they would receive lifetime security. By the 1960s, societal support for that concept was declining. It had taken a long time for women, as well as men, to absorb that reality, but the time had come to make long-awaited changes in the laws regarding the dissolution of marriage. The California Family Law Act of 1970 would soon transform the process of divorce in important ways.

CHAPTER TWENTY-SEVEN

B efore passage of the California Family Law Act of 1970 substantially changed the process of divorce, the plaintiff (the person who initiated the action) would file for divorce, setting forth her grounds for terminating the marriage. Adultery topped the list as the most frequently stated reason for divorce. It was seldom difficult to find evidence that the defendant, generally the husband, had committed adultery. He was then considered to be "at fault" for causing the divorce.

After passage of the Family Law Act on January 1, 1970, fault (including adultery and the other bases for divorce) was eliminated. As a result, community property was divided equally, alimony (based on fault) was eliminated, and spousal support was based on the supported spouse's need to retrain to become self-supporting.

Most people didn't comprehend the concept of no-fault divorce, because the model for marriage had long been "husband in the work force, wife at home." The Family Law Act erased that paradigm.

Although the basis for division of community property and the determination of alimony and spousal support changed dramatically, child custody and child support decisions did not. Nonetheless, several issues remained that created the basis for a contested dissolution of marriage, in addition to division of community property and spousal support. One involved separating the parties safely and another addressed child custody and the best interests of the child(ren).

With the inception of no-fault divorce, the spouse who initiated the procedure would file a petition for dissolution and request that the other spouse be ordered to leave the family residence. That matter would be heard within a month on a judicial procedure known as the "law and motion calendar" for family law.

As an attorney, I considered this event dangerous for the client. When I served as counsel for the petitioner, I would frequently ask for a home exclusion to exclude a potentially hostile spouse from having access to the home, but local judges often denied this request. That action put the client in a vulnerable position.

When discussing the issue with my client, we generally tried to arrange for an alternative location for her safety, if it appeared necessary. Alternatives included a temporary stay with a member of her extended family, residence in a shelter for battered women, or even a brief stay in a local hotel.

Immediately after filing the petition, we would schedule the matter for an upcoming court appearance to resolve temporary issues such as occupancy of the residence, restraining orders, spousal and child support, and custody of the children.

At this hearing, the judge would typically order the husband out of the house and direct him to provide support for the wife and children until the matter could be set on the trial calendar. The wife would almost always receive custody of the children.

Sometimes giving the wife custody was not the best choice. Early in my practice, I represented a physician husband who worked in the emergency room of a local hospital. He told me his wife had been driving in northern California a few years before, with the family in the car, when she suddenly stopped, ordered the husband and their three children out of the car, and then sped off. He and the children managed to return to San Mateo County but not without difficulty.

On another occasion, she slammed the car into the wall at the end of the garage, barely avoiding their youngest son, who had been standing in front of the car moments before. Although we brought these issues to the attention of the court, the judge ordered the husband out of the family residence rather than the wife.

Sometimes it appeared the judge found the matter so difficult to decide that he simply followed a script. No women judges existed at the time, and most judges decided in favor of the wife when considering child custody matters.

In another case in which my client was the husband, he had been the sole caretaker of the couple's son. He had cared for his son from infancy to fifteen years of age while continuing to fulfill his work obligations at the racetrack. The judge ordered custody of the then-teenaged boy to be given to the wife.

The young man refused to live with his mother and left to find his father at the track. We couldn't let the judge's order stand. I obtained an attorney for the boy, and he was able to have the erroneous child custody order reversed.

I often arranged for an improperly placed child to attend court with his/her own attorney. Otherwise, the dispute between the parents could become a matter of he said/she said, and the outcome might be disastrous for the child.

Another issue that created a contested action involved the valuation of the husband's business. For example, a lawyer in private practice would be in possession of a family asset that needed to be valued and divided. If the business was valued at $100,000 and the family residence was valued at the same amount, a judge might award the business to him and the house to her. Each party would likely hire an accountant as an expert witness. Thousands of dollars of attorney/accountant bills raised the cost of those dissolutions considerably.

The issue of the amount and length of time for payment of spousal support presented yet another basis for a contested case. Since I had spent decades in what I visualized as a boxing ring before I left to attend law school, I pursued this issue relentlessly on behalf of my clients. I did not have great success.

Often the client would be consumed by emotional problems surrounding the marital breakdown or the children who were caught up in the process. She often did not have the ability or desire to pursue higher education. Nevertheless, I was successful in getting a large enough order for spousal support so that one client, who had been a bookkeeper, could obtain her CPA.

Procedures in family law resembled those for other aspects of civil law. If a matter needed judicial intervention prior to trial, it would be placed on the law and motion calendar, roughly equivalent to the first appearance in the family law matter.

Depositions (the process of giving sworn testimony) in family law generally occurred if a contested issue arose. Interrogatories (written questions submitted to a party) were less expensive and often produced the same result.

Settlements could take place at any time and were usually required if the matter were scheduled for trial. Judges disliked trials in family law matters and would often go out of their way to help the parties settle the case.

When judges helped litigants settle a case, it took place within the court system. The parties reached an agreement, and they appeared in a court setting and recited the terms of the settlement. Then one of the attorneys prepared a formal document of Judgment of Dissolution of Marriage, along with the other provisions.

In an out-of-court settlement, the two attorneys worked together to get a Marital Settlement Agreement that could be attached to a Judgment of Dissolution. What was important was having the entire matter in writing and signed by a judge, which made it a Judgment of Dissolution of Marriage.

Issues settled during trials sometimes required further modification after the trial due to a change of circumstances. Frequently, these came from the husband (or supporting spouse), who sought to review spousal support orders made at the time of trial. Less frequently, either spouse might seek modification of a child custody issue.

The Family Law Act changed women's lives forever. Marriage no longer offered a lifetime-support guarantee, and many women were hurt by the modification. Most of their little girls grew up with the understanding that they would need to be in the marketplace for at least some portions of their lives.

The Family Law Act revolutionized not only women's lives but also the entire structure of the family.

CHAPTER TWENTY-EIGHT

Now let's look at our judicial system. Although each state is a part of the larger United States, certain areas, such as the judiciary, are reserved for the individual states. Federal and bankruptcy courts do exist, but the bulk of the system for dealing with individuals and corporations (which, as entities, are treated as individuals) lies with the states.

The process often starts in this manner: Local police stop a car for doing something they perceive as illegal, which can be as minor as driving with expired license tags on the vehicle. The matter may end there, especially if the person who was stopped apologizes to the officer, but that rarely happens. If you want a good outcome, it's wise to be nice and address the policeman as "Sir."

If the situation escalates, it is likely to lead to the police taking the person into custody and putting them in jail. In most California counties, the dozen (or sometimes hundreds) of folks arrested the previous night appear before the judge in an arraignment calendar the next morning. The district attorney decides if he wants to prosecute. If he does, the defendant is released on a promise to return for further court hearings. Sometimes, bail is set to secure the individual's return.

The judge may review the defendant's financial circumstances. If they seem dismal enough, the judge will appoint a public or private defender to represent the accused. The defendant generally pleads not guilty, and additional dates for settlement conferences and the trial are established.

At that time, the defendant (now the defender's client) and the attorney meet for planning. Often the lawyer and client elect to do further investigation. Larger defense firms may have their own investigative departments, or they can hire an outside firm to do the work. It would be impossible for lawyers to do their own investigating, as there is just too much other work to be done. One important task is determining the attitudes of potential jurors. For example, if a potential juror has plastered his/her car with political signs that read "Jail the Bums," defense counsel would likely excuse that juror.

During settlement conferences, the district attorney, defense counsel, and a judge examine the case. Many cases are settled via plea bargain at this juncture. In welfare fraud cases, for example, if the district attorney has charged the client with felonies, he might be willing to settle the case for a plea to one misdemeanor plus the restitution of what they perceive to be the overpayment. The restitution process was financially devastating to single mothers in East Palo Alto, and they did not perceive they had done anything wrong. Their alternative was a jury trial, which could involve a heavier sentence than the woman would receive from a plea bargain. Early in my career as a lawyer, I handled several cases in this manner.

As soon as I began my law practice, I applied for membership in the Private Defender Committee. San Mateo County did not have a public defender, the body that provides lawyers for indigent people accused of crimes. Instead, it assigned those cases to local lawyers who were members of the special panel of private defenders. My application was granted, and I devoted about half my time to criminal defense for several years.

After handling a few minor cases of drunk driving or drunk in public, I gravitated to representing women accused of welfare fraud. Almost all the cases involved African American women living in East Palo Alto. Welfare payments were granted to the mother if the father of a child was unemployed or absent from the home. If the welfare recipient started working, she was required to report her exact earnings to the county welfare department.

Many recipients failed to do so, thus creating an overpayment of welfare assistance. The result was a misdemeanor charge for an overpayment of less than $200 per month. However, if the amount exceeded that sum, a felony charge came into play. Not all counties followed that procedure. San Mateo was both unique and strict.

Occasionally, the facts of a case were more complicated.

For my first trial, I was the attorney for Verna Douglas, an African American woman with three children. She had no idea as to the location of the children's father, which made her eligible for welfare assistance. Her children included Angela, a sixteen-year-old pregnant girl; Bob, a twelve-year-old boy already in the throes of the justice system; and Charlie, a four-year-old boy who had not yet landed in trouble.

I perceived Verna as being so distraught about her life that she was unable to understand the reporting requirements for her welfare payments. She might also have been semi-literate. For the prosecutor to obtain a conviction for these misdemeanors, the action or inaction must be proven to be willful (deliberate or purposeful). The district attorney offered the standard plea bargain of guilty to one count and restitution of the perceived overpayment. We rejected the offer and proceeded to trial.

I did not have a jury consultant for that trial, so I was on my own. The judge called for the jury panel (people who had received a summons for jury duty) to enter the courtroom, and the clerk began a random selection. Both the prosecutor and I had an opportunity to challenge a juror "for cause." Such a challenge would be appropriate if the prosecutor's sister were in the jury pool and had been selected. Another challenge for cause would occur if the juror had a close connection to either counsel.

Assuming neither attorney challenged a juror for cause, the next step was a possible preemptory challenge (a challenge for any reason). When a potential juror was accepted, s/he would be seated in the jury box and the next potential juror called. That process continued until the jury selection was complete.

After three jurors had been seated in the Douglas trial, a woman was the next potential juror. After addressing her by name, I asked if she preferred being addressed as Miss, Mrs., or Ms. I didn't know whether the question was proper, and I imagined being held in contempt of court and jailed. I held my breath and waited. It had been only a few years since the prohibition against women jurors had been rejected by the United States Supreme Court.

She replied, "I prefer Ms." I took a deep breath, but my stomach turned. I could hardly continue. Somehow, I survived, and the twelve-person jury was seated.

The prosecution began with an opening statement. Defense counsel can make a statement at that time or reserve the right to do so later. We reserved the right to postpone our statement. Then the district attorney called witnesses and presented other evidence, including the welfare department's schedule of required and not-too-well-reported payments.

After each witness for the prosecution takes the stand, the defense can cross-examine him/her for the purpose of creating doubt about the district attorney's case. After the prosecution rests, the defense makes its own case, with its witnesses also subject to cross-examination. In the Douglas case, the district attorney presented a witness regarding the required payments and the non-reporting of the benefits. There was little to be gained by an extensive cross-examination of that prosecution witness.

New attorneys are instructed to advise clients not to take the stand. However, since our theory was incapacity and non-willful non-reporting, that paradigm would not be helpful in the Douglas case. I thought if Verna took the stand, her cross-examination would help her case.

I made my opening statement, which included a declaration that the defendant was so emotionally distraught that she could not do the required reporting. The prosecution presented its case and then rested.

I called Verna to the stand and asked if she had a problem with the older daughter. She said, "Yes." Then she explained that the young woman had gone into labor. She said she had barely arrived at the hospital by the time her daughter delivered the baby.

I asked about the trouble with her son. She described her efforts to keep him out of the judiciary system and admitted that her attempts had failed. Her testimony was overlaid with evidence of her panic and angst. The prosecution's cross-examination made clear her obvious inability to correctly report her income.

After summation by both attorneys, the jury retired. It seemed as if they would remain in deliberation forever, but they returned after a day and said they were hopelessly deadlocked. On the first and second charges, she was found not guilty 7-4. On the third count, she was found not guilty by a unanimous vote. She was found guilty on the fourth count 8-4. Thus, we had an acquittal on one count and a hung jury on three counts.

The prosecution can keep trying the case after a hung jury. However, in Verna's situation, the prosecution moved to dismiss the case. It was a major victory for us.

After the matter concluded, I made an appointment to see the judge about my performance. I expected him to tell me I didn't know section 4125 of the Evidence Code. (There is no such thing.) That kind of information might have been significant for the bar examination, but law school, the bar, and legal practice are all different. Instead, the judge said he thought the most important aspects of defendant representation were articulation and enunciation. He also said I was free to ask to approach the bench during a trial, and he would help.

I took him at his word. At my next trial with him as the judge, I ran up to the bench frequently. The jurors might have thought that meant I was inexperienced and naïve, but I won the case.

CHAPTER TWENTY-NINE

After I had established a reputation for representing defendants in welfare fraud cases, the case of Mary George, charged with five felonies between 1972 and 1975, was referred to me.

Mary was a single woman who lived in East Palo Alto. She had no children but had let her family know she wanted them. In the late 1950s, her sister had given her eighth child to Mary, saying she did not want him. Mary called the boy Johnny, and she embraced him with joy as his mother. The only blot on her happiness was the fact that he remained almost illiterate by the time he entered high school. I agreed with Mary's opinion that Johnny appeared to have normal learning capacity and that the Palo Alto School system had failed him.

Mary's brother, Richard, had married a white woman. Their union produced three children, Belle, Bobby, and Della, with whom the father had no relationship. The mother, who lived in Menlo Park, had such difficulty raising them that she simply gave up. Without warning, she and the children turned up at Mary's door. "I can't handle these children," she told Mary. "You take them."

It was a big responsibility but one that Mary accepted with delight. She applied for welfare payments for the children, which was granted. The money provided enough income to properly care for her growing family.

My client worried about where to send her nieces and nephew to school. After her experience with the quality of education in East Palo Alto, she was not willing to take a chance there. The children were already enrolled in school at Menlo Park, where their mother lived and had been receiving welfare assistance for them.

East Palo Alto is a warm community, where people help each other as they can. Mary didn't drive, so she asked a friend, Mr. Hall, to transport the children to and from school in Menlo Park. He did so for the nearly three years they lived with my client.

The case came to the attention of the local district attorney. They charged Mary, the defendant, with five felony counts. If she were to be found guilty, she would likely serve time in jail or even prison.

Mary and I discussed her situation, and we agreed that she would not accept a plea bargain under any circumstances. She had done nothing wrong. The children had lived with her, and Mary's welfare assistance had been used to care for them.

The private defender granted me a jury consultant named Wanda. She had information about almost everyone on the jury panel. We appeared for trial at the set time. The issue in all five counts was whether the children lived with Mary during the time she received welfare assistance payments for them.

The standard plea bargain offer appeared from the district attorney. Mary soundly rejected it. "We came here to prove the children were with me. Why would I cooperate with the prosecutors?" she said.

Theoretically, she was presumed innocent under the law, but from a practical point of view, she bore the burden of proving that she was entitled to the welfare grant for the children. That meant proving the children had lived with her.

With Wanda by my side, I selected the jury. The district attorney presented his short case. He established that the children attended Menlo Park schools (or were registered there) and that their mother received welfare payments for them. The prosecutor claimed that they lived with their mother.

The children's mother did not testify, but a few individuals did. The district attorney claimed the witnesses had knowledge of the facts. One woman testified that she had been the babysitter while the mother worked from 9:00 a.m. to 5:00 p.m. We suspected her claim was fraudulent.

At Wanda's suggestion, I sent a subpoena to the mother's place of employment and requested that the record keeper attend court and present the records of the mother's employment. They showed she had worked the night shift for several of the months involved. No one was at home during those hours, so she couldn't have had a daytime babysitter. When the record keeper appeared, I called her as a witness.

I had also scheduled as witnesses many of Mary's friends in East Palo Alto who had seen her and the children living together. I asked each witness about meals, bedrooms, toys, clothes, and other aspects of life for a family of five. Our case took a lot of time because for the thirty-six months involved, I asked each witness the same question for each month. For example, I would say, "In June of 1973, did you see them eating at Mary's house? Was it breakfast, lunch, and/or dinner?" The next-door neighbors were strong witnesses because they clearly saw and reported on almost all aspects of the five members of Mary's household.

Particularly important was the testimony of the driver, Mr. Hall, who had transported the children to and from school every day from East Palo Alto to Menlo Park and back.

One of my most crucial witnesses was the milkman. Mary and Johnny had received enough milk for one adult woman and a young man for many months before the arrival of Belle, Bobby, and Della. After the children arrived, her milk deliveries increased to accommodate three additional children. The deliveries were substantially reduced when the children returned to their mother sometime in 1975.

I decided not to call Mary as a witness. I just couldn't put her through that ordeal. Standard procedure for defense attorneys is not to call the client to testify. This theory derives from the Fifth Amendment to the Constitution: No one is required to be a witness against himself.

What is likely to happen when the defendant testifies is that she, as innocent as she might be, will incriminate herself. There would likely be much twisting and turning of her testimony, and the client may become angry and exhibit an emotion that attorneys do not want clients to demonstrate to the jury. Angry people are not likeable, and it is important for the jury to like the defendant. In this case, we had enough witnesses to the children's residence. Mary's testimony was not necessary, and it was not worth the risk.

The term *summing up* describes the opportunity for both the prosecution and defense to summarize their theory of the case and the testimony of their witnesses. They then make an argument for their position to the jury. Both the prosecutor and I gave our speeches. Mine took a long time since I had asked every witness the same set of questions.

Some people believe I would have been nervous during the trial, but I didn't have time. I had to keep calm and think about what I was doing every single second. Mary and I talked about her case as often as possible, and we felt satisfied with the way it was progressing.

The jury went out on a Friday morning. They called to have the milkman's testimony reread and then retired to deliberate further.

I returned to my office to consult briefly with Leo, my office mate and long-time mentor. I felt unsettled about the obviously fraudulent witness who testified that she had babysat the children when she couldn't possibly have done so. Leo told me I should keep my mouth shut. He said whenever a jury is out, anything that interrupts their deliberations is counterproductive.

I returned to the courthouse, and Mary and I held our breath. She was upset not because she could go to prison but because the prosecution had interfered with her relationship with what she viewed as her children. They had become remarkably close.

In the middle of the afternoon, the jury called to say they had a verdict. The judge looked at each juror individually as they filed into the courtroom. Just loudly enough for the court clerk, court reporter, and both attorneys to hear, he said, "They are going to acquit." And, indeed, they did. On each count, each juror said, "Not guilty."

We sat there for a moment, stunned. The high emotions I couldn't allow myself to experience during the trial exploded, and I started to shake. Mary and her friend said, "Let's go."

It was over. The judge said, "Good luck."

Later, a friend told me the judge commented that I'd done a nice job.

I had developed a good reputation within the county. If I didn't know it before, I knew it then: I was meant to be a lawyer.

CHAPTER THIRTY

I found the treatment of women litigants and women attorneys to be unacceptable not only in San Mateo County but also throughout the state. As soon as I started practicing, I decided I would address the issue every time it presented itself. Dozens of opportunities appeared.

I joined the San Francisco Women Lawyers Club, known as Queen's Bench, and began to work toward becoming an officer on the board of directors. Several members who practiced family law created a committee we called the Women and the Law Committee. The San Mateo County Bar Association graciously welcomed us.

Perhaps a year later, Burt Bloomstead, an attorney who practiced a significant amount of family law and was already a friend, invited colleagues to a family law function. While the gathering was a good idea, he scheduled the function at a men's restaurant, and any woman attorney who arrived was rejected at the door. I called Burt about it, and he could not have been more apologetic. He scheduled the next meeting at a local gender-neutral restaurant.

We then formed the San Mateo Family Law Committee, and again the bar was pleased to accept us. I did much of the work on the committee during Burt's year of chairing it. Other female lawyers helped, including members of the Women and the Law Committee. I invited them to join Queen's Bench as well. We became a formidable group within the bar association.

After serving for a year on the Family Law Committee, Burt recommended that I be named the next chair. I accepted and decided to ask all the superior court judges, one at a time, to speak at our monthly meetings. Few of them knew much about the ways the Family Law Act had changed family law, so it was an opportunity for each of them to learn about it and update their knowledge base.

Burt introduced me at the next meeting. I formally accepted the position of committee chair and told the story of the first meeting at the men-only restaurant. Then I said, "The story demonstrates how bar association meetings and sex are similar." I paused until I had everyone's attention. Once the room became quiet, I said, "Whatever it is you are trying to do, it is ever so much better if both the man and the woman are active participants."

Everyone laughed. Locally, at least on a temporary basis, both committees had struck a positive tone.

My plan to become an officer in Queen's Bench met with success from the time I opened my office. I was named assistant secretary-treasurer in my first year and held the position for two years. The nominating committee then asked me to move into the vice presidency.

A few days later, however, I was notified there would be another nomination from the floor. I was moving rapidly, working toward making Queen's Bench into a lawyer's feminist organization. A small group of queen bees who had dominated the organization for years didn't like it.

They had misjudged me. After twenty years in the boxing ring, I was not to be pushed aside. I organized a campaign and won.

During my vice presidency, in addition to the normal duties of the office, I organized and presented a forum that I called "The Women in the Courtroom Conference." Several panels formed, as women boasted one or two active participants in almost every specialty, including family law, criminal law, and workers compensation. We also presented a judge's panel. In 1975, San Francisco, the East Bay, and Marin had eight municipal court judges. Santa Clara County had one superior court judge.

The conference led Queen's Bench to petition the new governor, Jerry Brown, to appoint women to all California courts. Rose Bird, Chief Justice of the California Supreme Court, became his first appointment, and he followed her with many others.

In those days, the VP was nominally president-elect, and my presidency occurred almost uneventfully. Before and just after my presidency began, two cases involving women as a class were moving through the court system and up to the California Supreme Court. The first involved the issue of a man and woman living together and behaving as if they were married when they were not. The precedent (the prior law that had to be followed) was that the courts leave the parties as it had found them. In general, that meant the court left the woman impoverished and the man wealthy. Although the issue wasn't popular in Queen's Bench, I felt strongly that we couldn't ignore it.

The Queen's Bench board approved my request to petition the California Supreme Court to serve as *amicus curiae* for Michelle Triola Marvin in the case of *Marvin v. Marvin*. *Amicus curiae* literally means *friend of the court*. In other words, we said to the court, "This is not just a matter of the two litigants. It has broader societal issues of which we would like the court to be aware." A few women professors at statewide law schools also petitioned and were approved as *amici*.

The outcome of *Marvin v Marvin* 18 Cal 3rd 665 (1976) was favorable to our cause. The court treated the parties not as family law litigants but as parties to an oral contract. Personally, I was delighted. *Marvin* was the case I would have brought on my own behalf if Sherwin had not elected to honor our agreement.

The Family Law Act changed the "rules" for marriage for women in 1970. Another issue was on its way to the Supreme Court. Unlike *Marvin*, that case was more closely related to family law itself in that trial courts and appellate courts had been denying spousal support to women who had married for lifetime security. In the *Morrison* case, Mrs. Morrison was originally awarded minimum support, which was set to terminate after a few years. We thought the court should seek jurisdiction to make another award when the support ended.

We hired Gertrude Chern, a close friend and appellate specialist, to act as *amici* for Queen's Bench. The court ruled: "The trial court must retain jurisdiction to make an award of spousal support after a lengthy marriage unless the record shows that she would be able to provide for herself at the time set for termination."

We had won the case. Those of us who had worked on the brief were overjoyed, and we gathered for a well-deserved celebration.

CHAPTER THIRTY-ONE

One of the first events in my Queen's Bench presidency involved the long-standing dinner for local judges, during which the organization honored its incoming president. My turn came in early 1976, just after my installation as president.

Since becoming a Queen's Bench member, I had invited many of the members of the San Mateo County Women and the Law Committee to join the Bench. Somehow, the local board of directors of the San Mateo bar became confused as to who was hosting the dinner. For several days before their board meeting, rumors circulated that the Women and the Law Committee had initiated the action.

The awkward situation could have been resolved easily had the bar president called me to clarify the situation. He did not do so, and I couldn't let them pass judgment on something that was essentially none of their business.

I wrote the following letter:

Dear Mr. President,

It is my understanding that significant rumors have been circulating to the effect that the Women and the Law Committee has inappropriately asked local judges to a dinner. I am reluctant to respond to rumors; however, in this situation, with all due respect, I must communicate that your information is incorrect.

Queen's Bench, the Bay Area organization to promote the interests of women in the legal profession and the judiciary, is slightly older than the San Mateo County Bar Association, both having been formed in the late twenties. Throughout the history of Queen's Bench, the incoming president has been recognized by hosting a dinner in her honor for the local judiciary.

I am the incoming president of Queen's Bench, having assumed office in late January. Queen's Bench is hosting the dinner for the local judges. I am hopeful that this explanation will clarify the situation.

YVT
Ruth Miller, President, Queen's Bench

He responded appropriately, and we had a lovely dinner with the local judges.

During the period from 1971 through 1976, I had created committees, joined organizations, and accepted appointments to groups of lawyers who sought equality for women within the bar, the judiciary, and society itself. Most important was my selection for the State Bar Family Law Committee. We met once a month on a Saturday, alternating between a San Francisco airport hotel and its counterpart in Los Angeles. Those meetings provided opportunities to interact with lawyers from all over the state and learn how differently family law was practiced in each county.

In 1975, the committee held a holiday meeting over a full weekend at Catalina Island. One of our discussions at that meeting focused on legal specialization. Family law suffered from a terrible reputation when I started practice. In my opinion, the unfortunate reputation stemmed from the fact that one-half of family law clients were women. In addition, after The Family Law Act, it wasn't clear how lawyers were to get paid. That concern certainly contributed to the negative perception of family law. If we were to improve the status of the specialty, we would need to correct the compensation problem.

In 1972, the State Bar had initiated a pilot program for legal specialization. Lawyers practicing criminal law, workers' compensation, and tax law could apply to become specialists in their field. Certain rules applied, including the number of trials the budding specialists would have to complete and specific education requirements.

Endless discussions ensued as to whether a lawyer's membership in a state bar specialization program would indicate competence. I considered that issue irrelevant. What I deemed important to a potential client was whether the lawyer was interested in the field in which s/he sought specialization. That had not been the case in family law. Many a lawyer had told me he could hardly wait to gain success in other fields so he didn't have to "do domestic." Any lawyer like the one my client Lois had initially retained would be an attorney I would not like to have. He would never go through the ropes to become a specialist in family law because he felt it was beneath him.

At the meeting on Catalina Island, I raised the issue of family law as a certified specialty. Electric waves crackled around the room at my suggestion. Everyone there seemed to believe it was a good idea. In the end, the one issue upon which we all agreed was that making family law a specialty would raise its standing within the legal profession. *Hurray!*

We knew that we could not achieve our goal without subjecting potential specialists to a written examination. The pilot program was over. The committee appointed me and another member to draft standards for family law certified specialists.

On the day after Mary George was acquitted, I drove to the central valley of California to meet with the other committee member to compile a set of proposed rules for family law certification. After the committee at large approved them, we sent the proposed rules to the Board of Legal Specialization, accompanied by a request that family law join the three other specialties.

I followed up on the project for several months, always hearing that the matter was pending. Then one day I heard from the president of the board. He asked me if I would chair the newly formed subcommittee to be known as The Family Law Advisory Commission to the Board of Legal Specialization." The purpose would be to explore family law as a certified specialty. I didn't hesitate when I said, "Yes!"

The matter dragged through various committees, including the Board of Legal Specialization and the State Bar Board of Directors for years. The details, the arguments, and the entire issue were masticated repeatedly, but we finally prevailed. In 1979, family law became the fourth certified specialty.

Our work had not ended. We had to write the examination and correct it. Our committee, made up of members who had worked hard to create the specialty, could not take an examination we had written, so we hired a company to write an examination for us. Each committee member would have been embarrassed if we had failed, but we all passed.

Apart from my law practice and my efforts on behalf of women in the legal profession, I had spent about seven years creating, organizing, and managing family law as a certified specialty. It was my baby. That specialty is now over thirty years old and has enjoyed success beyond what any of us imagined possible.

Whenever I wonder if my life has been worthwhile, remembering what we accomplished reminds me it has. Nothing could have given me more joy or been more worthwhile for women in our society than this project. When I see the plethora of women in high positions today, I feel a deep sense of satisfaction. I know our work formed the foundation for significantly improving the status of women in society, specifically in the late twentieth century.

Since the beginning of humankind, men have dominated women, which has worked to women's disadvantage. There was little that most women could do, particularly while under the burden of bearing and raising so many children. The lone feminist was truly alone. Susan B. Anthony endured much negativity and hostility and probably led an unhappy life.

That paradigm died in the 1960s by virtue of two intertwining events: the development of the pill, a more effective method of birth control than previously existed, and the Family Law Act, which ended the assumption of lifetime support. An independent existence became possible for any woman who wanted it.

In my own life, I had escaped from the boxing ring. It made me not only free but fearless. After I became a lawyer, every time I encountered misogyny, I also found eager supporters to help me challenge it. When Burt invited men only to his family law luncheon, and I called him on it, his reaction was apologetic, not antagonistic.

Society was ready to accept women. Together, we changed the world.

CHAPTER THIRTY-TWO

L awyers do not inspire adoration unless it's their own. That truth became complicated by the certification of family law attorneys, which created a new and intricate body of law. Few members of the public recognized this fact, and many approached their own cases with an arrogant attitude. Frank was such a person.

He had responded to his wife's petition for dissolution of marriage with the conviction that he didn't need "any fancy lawyer." Property division was minimal, and Frank chose to proceed without counsel.

His wife had better sense. Her lawyer drafted an agreement that contained these two conflicting paragraphs:

1. Spousal support is awarded for five years. The court retains jurisdiction to make a further award if, at time set for termination, the court finds that (the supported spouse) is unable to care for herself.

2. Spousal support is awarded for five years after which time it shall absolutely terminate.

The first item reflected *Morrison* language, while the second introduced a conflicting order that directly opposed an important aspect of the first.

Frank signed the agreement and paid the support ordered. His former wife called him at the end of the five-year period and announced that she wanted payments to continue indefinitely. Immediately thereafter, he scheduled an appointment with me.

"What's the deal?" he asked. "The agreement says, 'Spousal support shall absolutely terminate after five years.'"

I looked over the paperwork and asked, "Did you read the paragraph just above the one you are relying on?"

Frank said, "Oh, that doesn't mean anything."

Our discussion continued for about fifteen minutes, during which I pointed out that the first paragraph meant the support may or may not terminate, which allows the court to have another look at the situation at the end of five years.

Frank shifted in his seat, and his entire body tensed. "How could this have happened to me?" he asked. "Why didn't the lawyer tell me?"

I sighed and stated the obvious. "You were your own lawyer."

I sensed the change in his emotions as they moved from outrage to exasperation to fear and finally to understanding.

"So I guess I goofed. Can you do anything for me now?"

"Yes," I said. "But we probably won't win this next hearing. You need to trust me and believe that I know what I am doing. Correcting this will not be easy; it will take a lot of work.

He agreed and gave me the go-ahead.

At the time of the hearing, the judge extended support for another two years and then terminated it with a further retention of jurisdiction. Frank's initial reaction was anger, but he remembered my prediction and his promise to trust me.

We moved forward. I took his former wife's deposition and asked if she had done anything to seek employment or train for a new position. She had done nothing. Then I referred her to a career counselor for evaluation, which revealed that she was able to earn nearly $2,000 per month. At the next hearing, based on the testimony of the career counselor, I was able to show the court that Frank's former spouse had the ability to care for herself. The judge terminated the support.

Frank was one of the most grateful clients I have ever served.

I discussed the outcome of his case with colleagues, and we all agreed that the upheaval in men's and women's relationships was so massive that it would take years, if not decades, for us to absorb the impact.

In addition to *Marvin* and *Morrison*, several other issues became formal positions within the body of family law. Those included (1) imputation of income, (2) the method for handling a down payment on a spouse's separate property into a community property residence, and (3) alternate values of property (i.e., whether to value income or assets as of the date of separation).

Regarding the first issue, it was not uncommon for one or both spouses to attempt to alter either income or the value of assets in their own favor during the period of separation. They would certainly want to make any changes before they went to trial for a final division of assets and establishment of more lengthy periods of support.

Some clever individuals suggested that support be set at the amount it had been for each party prior to the petition for dissolution of marriage. For example, if the husband had been earning $60,000 at the date of separation, he could immediately quit or be dismissed from his job and claim he was only earning $40,000. He could then ask that child and spousal support be based on the lower figure. From those facts, the theory of "imputation of income" arose.

In the late 1990s, a complex case came to my office. My client, Wilma, had been earning about $25,000 per year as a therapist. Harry, her former husband, was a lawyer who worked in corporate law and earned $115,000 per year. They had two children, and child support was set at the level scheduled for that set of incomes.

Harry didn't like corporate law, so he left his job and went to work for a public defender, where he earned $90,000 per year. Wilma remarried, ended gainful employment, and added two more children to her family. Harry became angry that he had to continue support for *his* children at the same level. I told his attorney, who had petitioned for a reduction of child support, that Wilma, my client, would oppose his motion. I added that we would seek support based on the theory of imputation of income and ask the court to deny his motion.

Harry fired his lawyer and came to court *in pro per* (as his own lawyer). I imagined that his attorney had described my theory, and Harry's reply was along the line of "That's crazy!"

He made his presentation in court, asking that child support be reduced because Wilma had reduced her income level to zero. I pointed out to the court that he also had reduced his income from $115,000 to $90,000.

The judge interrupted me and asked Harry, "Is that true?"

He said, "Yes." He explained that he had wanted to do something more significant with his law practice, and being a public defender aligned with that goal.

I pointed out that the social value of his becoming a public defender was no more an issue than the personal value of Wilma's career choices. I said, "Both of these litigants have reduced their annual incomes by $25,000 since the time of their trial. If income is to be imputed to her, it should also be imputed to him."

The judge agreed with me, saying, "If I am to impute income to one of the parties, I should treat the other similarly."

The next time I talked with Harry's former attorney, I had to be careful not to parade my glee about the outcome of the case.

The second significant issue in family law concerned what happens to a separate property down payment into an otherwise community-property house. Some courts ignored it altogether, and one party lost all of his/her down payment. Some returned it to the "separator" at the original value. Others returned it with either interest or appreciation when the house was sold.

After much litigation, the California legislature resolved the matter by enacting a law to return the down payment without interest or appreciation to the spouse who had owned the separate property. The decision enabled family law attorneys to provide solid legal advice to our clients.

Sometime after the enactment of The Family Law Act, it became obvious to me that changing the law by legislation is faster than going through litigation, with its many courts and conflicting decisions, which require a resolution for each case.

While I chaired the State Bar Family Law Committee, I addressed the third issue by proposing that we petition the legislature to value assets not at the date of trial but at the time of separation, which would reduce the opportunity for one or both spouses to alter the assets. The committee approved.

After bouncing around the internal structure of the state bar, the issue became a state bar sponsored matter before the California legislature. The issue was set for a debate at the legislature in August of 1976. If I wanted the new law to pass, I knew I must be there to testify.

I arrived for my testimony before the appropriate legislative body in Sacramento, which was slated for two o'clock in the afternoon. The legislators appeared conflicted about the proposal. After an internal discussion, they decided to approve the proposal with this addition: "On motion, and for good cause shown, the court may value any or all of the assets at the date of separation."

With that, the matter became law.

CHAPTER THIRTY-THREE

My law practice intensified my awareness that gender conflict and the role of women in society had been in upheaval since the passage of The Family Law Act. However, I had seen only the modern version of what had been a centuries-long fight during which the structure of divorce and divorce laws radically changed the status of women in society. By 1989, I wanted to understand my contemporary observations in much greater historical detail.

Two well-known institutions offered PhD programs for lawyers in the San Francisco Bay Area. Big obstacles existed at both institutions, including a requirement that I leave my law practice, which I was unwilling to do. As an interim step, I taught a business law course at the State University of California at San Jose, where I discovered the Fielding Institute (now Fielding Graduate University).

Fielding offered advanced degrees in an individual course of study. I was admitted to their program in late 1989 and chose "Alimony and Divorce: An Historical-Comparative Study of Gender Conflict" as my dissertation topic. After five years of study, I earned my PhD.

My first step toward that degree involved a review of the entire history of divorce within the literature, that is, everything written on the subject. Then I reviewed 142 years of high-conflict divorce in Colusa County, California, discovering that the history of divorce has been the fight of individual women, first for their lives and then for their safety, sanity, and status.

The men I read about had employed knives, razors, axes, and guns against their wives. When they did not have weapons readily available, they used their feet and fists. They attempted to choke, seriously disable, or otherwise manipulate their wives with threats.

Without the sexual pairing that began with Adam and Eve, humanity would not have survived. Marriage, as we know it, developed through Christianity as an indissoluble sacrament. When Protestantism arose in the sixteenth century, society began to experiment with divorce.

Neuchatel, Switzerland, converted to Protestantism in 1530. Divorce became available immediately, but in a form that would not be satisfactory by today's standards. A woman who was abandoned by her husband would need to remain chaste indefinitely. Any violation could cause her to forfeit all her worldly possessions.

At one point in Neuchatel, both parties had to be sexually functional, a condition that had to be proved by a physician, to obtain a divorce. The wife of a man named Abram sought a divorce, and the surgeons found that his sex organs were well formed. He therefore had to prove his sexual ability by having an erection in front of a witness. He pled illness the first time, and the committee postponed the event until he returned to health. He chose to let his wife have a divorce rather than be humiliated again.

After the Protestant revolution, England became the only Protestant country to forbid divorce. Sixteenth-century England swung so violently between Catholicism and Protestantism that many on the "wrong" (or opposite) side lost their heads. The threat of beheading may have contributed to the prohibition of divorce. However, as property rights were a significant factor in societal standing, society could not tolerate a wife's adultery. If it did, the bloodline could become contaminated, causing substantial confusion as to the proper heir in a family.

Between 1672 and 1857, Parliament granted 320 divorces to men who petitioned and three to women. The basis for the women's divorces were egregious. In two cases, the husband had committed adultery with his wife's sister. In the third case, Arthur Battersby lived with his wife for three weeks while openly visiting brothels. He gave her a venereal disease, left her, and married another woman. Battersby was subsequently convicted of and deported for bigamy.

Alternatives to divorce before 1857 included the murder, sale, and suicide of wives. After Parliament enacted the Divorce and Matrimonial Causes Act, divorce could be permitted only on grounds of adultery. As happened in California in 1970, when the law was changed on "procedural grounds," the structure of gender conflict and the status of women became radically altered.

In colonial America, the so-called land of the free and home of the brave, divorce appeared to be easier for women than in England or Protestant parts of Europe. In Massachusetts, grounds for divorce were based on Puritan values. Consanguinity (being related by blood), bigamy, impotency, and adultery could serve as grounds for divorce for either spouse. Connecticut followed similar laws.

On the other hand, ease of divorce became more difficult when America adopted the common law of England, as articulated by Englishman William Blackstone. He stated that "The civil and legal existence of the wife is suspended during marriage." Essentially, a woman became a nonperson when she married. The United States Supreme Court agreed with that theory as late as 1904, as recorded in a somewhat unrelated case. Occasionally, a court would deny the wife a divorce based upon her status of nonbeing, which meant the court had no jurisdiction to consider her complaint.

Most states followed the common law of England, but several followed civil law, derived from the Visigoths in early Spain. This group of people had expanded by slowly conquering neighboring territories, with the participation of both men and women. Men fought the battles and then went home to a lunch prepared by their wives. Gradually, the women became part of a community that entitled them to half the property acquired by the male soldiers. California, Texas, Washington, and a few other states followed the civil law theory rather than Blackstone's common law.

The community property system regarding marital property differed from the common law in that all property acquired after marriage, with the exception of gifts and inheritances, became "common property." Accordingly, the property of a woman of wealth remained her separate property when she married. California adopted this system as law in 1849. One commentator at the time noted that civil law, if enacted, would attract women of wealth to California and become an advantage for the state.

In addition to the concepts articulated by Blackstone and Puritanism, which were somewhat inconsistent with each other, the idea of divorce was generally unpopular in colonial America. The theory was that the family unit created by marriage was the smallest governmental division in society. If divorce were available, it would weaken society. It never seemed to occur to them that when a breakdown occurs in a small division of society such that a smaller group asks the larger group for dissolution, the little group makes the larger group not stronger but weaker.

In California, grounds for divorce resembled those in other states: impotence, adultery, extreme cruelty, willful neglect, willful desertion, and certain acts that are now the basis for annulment, such as marriage by fraud or force. Also adopted were so-called defenses to divorce, which became so technical that they produced extensive litigation.

One example, which reversed the trial court's grant of divorce to the plaintiff, is *Crim v. Crim* 66 Or.258 (1913), in which the Oregon Supreme court said, "A careful examination

... convinces us that the plaintiff is not free from fault." From this case and others, we realize that the issue was whether the divorce itself would be granted. Although Mrs. Crim had convinced the trial court of her position, she was out of luck at the appellate court, which reversed the trial court and denied the divorce.

The cases that best reveal historical gender conflict are those involving the grounds of extreme cruelty. They also demonstrate how the intensity of cruelty necessary for an uncontested divorce lessened as time advanced. In California, cruelty initially included both mental and physical distress. Name-calling emerged as grounds for divorce and grew like a plague. Terms such as "liar, damned liar, a damned old whore, a devil, the biggest old devil that God Almighty ever let live, and an old heifer" were listed, along with "others of a like opprobrious character."

Going beyond name-calling, one husband claimed his wife tried to poison him and was intimate with another man. A strong double standard existed between what a woman versus a man had to prove to obtain a divorce.

The law included several concepts as a defense to divorce. Their absurdity often reached the level of nonsense. "Connivance" meant the defendant consented to the acts of the plaintiff.

"Collusion" referred to an agreement between the parties that the defendant would consent to the acts of the plaintiff to allow the plaintiff to obtain the divorce. For collusion to be successful, the defendant must have had a change of mind. A type of collusion, long popular in New York, occurred when a woman (who had been hired to play the part) would be found in her slip with the defendant. The wife could then claim the grounds of adultery to obtain a divorce.

"Condonation" involved the conditional forgiveness of an offense during the marriage that could serve as the grounds for divorce. The statute includes four technical aspects that the defendant must include to be successful in having the court deny the divorce.

"Recrimination," the epitome of divorce defense absurdity, occurred when the defendant was shown to have engaged in "any cause of divorce against the plaintiff, which would bar the plaintiff's cause of action."

Clearly, a conflict existed between the growing demand for divorce and the theory of the family as a unit of society. The California legislature believed that government was obligated to make divorce difficult. Fortunately, I found only one case that employed defenses to divorce (other than a denial of the plaintiff's complaint) during my review of the Colusa County cases.

By the mid-twentieth century, the California Supreme Court resolved the issue of making divorce difficult by awarding each party his/her own decree in *DeBurgh v. DeBurgh* 39 Cal 2nd 858 (1952). This case ended the practice of applying different standards to men versus women and hinted at the upcoming egalitarianism in this area, which arrived with the Family Law Act.

In retrospect, while technically available, divorce in California, from inception to *DeBurgh*, was often so complex that if the defendant wanted to contest it, s/he would likely succeed. Thus, the primary problem for women was the loss of support.

More complicated than the issue of divorce itself was the issue of how a woman who married in good faith and was tossed out by her husband in midlife would care for herself.

That issue remains unresolved today.

SECTION 6:

LIFE OUTSIDE THE
PRACTICE OF LAW

CHAPTER THIRTY-FOUR

Much in my life progressed smoothly while I practiced law and concentrated on improving the status of women. Floyd asked me to marry him, and although I declined at the time, our status of inseparability continued. He supported everything I did.

In 1973, I moved to the San Francisco Peninsula to be near my law practice while he remained in San Francisco. His career had gone well, but he chose to leave his position as an executive in the real estate company after ten years. I upgraded to a townhouse in Foster City, and he took an apartment in Pacifica. He—and his support of me—were perfect, and I adored every minute we spent together.

When I moved to San Francisco, none of my children wanted to leave their schools and lives in Tiburon, so they stayed with their father until they graduated from high school. When I left Tiburon, Nevin was nearly twelve years old, Stefani almost eight, and Trevis six.

At first, I spent every weekend with all three of my children, but by the time Nevin was a teenager, he had stopped spending weekends in San Francisco with me. I felt disappointed, but his agenda had diverged from mine, so I conceded without anger. I had read many articles about the conflicts common to relationships between mothers and their teenaged sons. Nevin apologized to me for his behavior some decades later, and he was astonished to learn that someone had already written about it.

I gave Stefani art lessons on Saturdays and offered golf lessons to all three. If they agreed to golf, then I played too. I was nearly forty years old, so I did not do as well as they did.

Although client and committee work required a great deal of time and attention, I prioritized spending time with my children as well. In addition to our weekends together, I took them on a vacation about once a year, and I treasure those memories.

We had done so well traveling to Arizona the previous year that we chose Mexico as our destination in 1973. We rented a larger vehicle for the ambitious trip, and Nevin's friend Derrick joined the four of us.

We stayed overnight in Mexicali so we could fill the motor home with gas, water, and other pertinent fluids. We had already stocked up on food and supplies and had assembled the appropriate paperwork, including specialized Mexican insurance, a necessity for traveling safely in Mexico.

Our primary stop was Guaymas. We parked the motor home and walked to the beach, where a group of residents were preparing to kill and cook a turtle for dinner. Stefani pleaded with me to save his life, but I couldn't do it. We had no way to get a large turtle off the beach, let alone across the border. I also had no interest in confronting a group of locals on their home turf.

Nevin and Derrick spent the first night on the roof of the motor home and were both bitten by an unidentified insect. They complained about the bites, but they didn't appear serious. The boys slept inside the RV after that, and a few days later, the mysterious bite marks had disappeared.

The trouble-seeking pair then created a "bomb" by digging a hole, filling it with explosives, and covering it with sand. After the detonation, nothing happened, so Derrick moved closer to inspect the device at the exact moment it exploded. He was showered with sand and one eye had taken on a red hue. I worried that he'd blinded himself.

After we rinsed the eye thoroughly, Derrick insisted he could see just fine, and we decided it would heal. No one else had been close enough to be injured.

When Nevin and Derrick grew bored, they teased Trevis mercilessly. One day, they told him he needed to clean out the sewer system in the RV. The system was connected to a hose that automatically drained it into a receptacle made for that purpose, so manual cleaning wasn't required. Trevis didn't know that, and the more he objected to their demands, the more they pressured him. Eventually, I had to intercede on my younger son's behalf.

In 1974, I rented a motor home so we could travel to the Grand Canyon in Arizona for a week. The children had been growing and maturing so fast, but they were still young enough to be affectionate and loving. They tugged at my heart during the whole trip. I loved them so much.

All three were excited at the prospect of trekking through the Grand Canyon. We listened to the instructions of the staff at the visitor center and learned that hiking the mile to the bottom of the canyon would require only a little energy. Then they added a warning that we might not be able to make the trek back up, which often happened to visitors. We walked only a little way down and then decided to turn back and head to our camp. Even though we didn't make it to the bottom, we thoroughly enjoyed the adventure.

On the way home, we stopped at Death Valley. We stayed in a formal campground, where the children discovered an abandoned cockapoo puppy. The campground staff gave us permission to "adopt" her. We called her Pepper, short for Salt and Pepper, which was a more accurate description. Pepper played an important part in the children's lives for many years.

Also in 1974, Sherwin and I scheduled a trip to Europe for the whole family. Stefani, Trevis, and I flew out of San Francisco on August 5, two days before Trevis's twelfth birthday. We had timed our departure so we could get a half-price ticket for him. Stefani was already over thirteen.

The three of us checked into a hotel on the west bank in Paris and spent several days exploring the area and seeing the sights. Next, we boarded a train for the Scandinavian countries, sleeping on the train for several nights. Trevis was still young enough that he had not absorbed the concept of tact or manners. He bluntly asked some folks from Amsterdam about their lives during World War II. I don't think any of us expected the answer they gave us. They said they couldn't get enough to eat. Feeling awkward, I extended our condolences. What else could I say?

We traveled south to meet Sherwin and his party in Rome. Sherwin's father had died the previous year, so his mother accompanied the group, along with Sherwin's friend Mary. Sherwin had flown to Europe with Mary, his mother, and Nevin about two weeks before Stefani, Travis, and I left the US.

After we arrived in Rome, the seven of us had lunch together and talked about all the places we had visited. The children and I then spent the afternoon at the Roman Colosseum. We were to meet the others at the airport bus station, where I was expected to hand over the children to Sherwin and his group and then fly home alone.

When Sherwin and I planned the trip, I had pleaded with him to buy tickets on two separate planes so all three children would not be on the same airplane. At first, he assured me he would, and then he added, "If it is convenient."

I knew what that meant. He would not do what I'd asked. I spent the next several hours in a dismal mood.

Nevin had apparently heard our conversation. He was in the throes of his first love and wanted to return home with me. Nevin and I talked about it, and I agreed to accommodate his desire.

Sherwin and his party arrived late at the meeting place, so we did not have time to discuss the matter in a leisurely manner. In fact, we had about two minutes before the group had to leave for their next European destination. Stefani and Travis headed to the bus, where the balance of the party was already seated.

Nevin stayed behind and said, "Dad, give me my passport and my ticket. I am going home with Mom." An argument seemed imminent, but Sherwin knew he couldn't risk missing his flight. So Nevin flew home with me.

Sherwin refused to speak to me for several years. He resented me for the part I had played in depriving him of his son's company during the remainder of that trip. His resentment became so great that he tried to take the children away from me permanently. Leo, my law partner, set him straight. However, when my next visit with the children approached, Sherwin said I could have them at one minute after midnight, the beginning of the next day.

In 1975, work and family intersected when the Family Law Committee held a holiday meeting over a full weekend at Catalina Island. I took Stefani and Trevis with me. They were strong swimmers, my having taught them to swim in our pool in Tiburon. While we attended meetings, my children enjoyed playing in the pool with the children of other committee members.

Our next big trip took place in 1976. I had scheduled the trip before I learned that I would be testifying in Sacramento on the first day of our vacation. I had shepherded the important bill, which proposed valuing assets at the time of marital separation rather than at the date of the trial, through the State Bar committees and the California Legislature. It was crucial that I appear before the legislators.

I rented a motor home, and we drove to Sacramento. Stefani had received her learner's permit six months before she qualified for a full driver's license. She asked me to let her drive the RV on the first leg of our journey, and I cautiously agreed. I was astonished at how very well she drove, and I complimented her skill in driving on the narrow two-lane mountain roads on the way to Idaho. She said, "I only did what I learned how to do in driving school."

We reached Lewiston, Idaho, the day after the hearing in Sacramento. After an overnight stay in Lewiston, the tour guide escorted us to central Oregon for our three-day trip down the Snake River. The rafting process was highly regulated, so our leaders could take the trip only once every three days. The tour guide barbequed dinner for us and made sure we ate a good breakfast and lunch.

Before we could enter the raft, our guides gave us detailed instructions to ensure our safety. Whenever we approached rapids, the guides asked us to exit the raft and walk around them while the staff brought the boat safely through. Then we'd reboard the raft and ride it until the next rapids loomed. It was quite the adventure, and we all enjoyed the exciting experience.

The next day, we crossed into Washington and drove up the coast and into Canada. We toured Butchart gardens and other well-known sightseeing landmarks, and we played many rounds of golf on beautifully manicured courses in scenic settings.

Stefani and I alternated driving on the trek back to the Bay Area, where I reluctantly returned Stefani and Trevis to their father's home. It was always painful to say goodbye to them after each trip, but I treasured every adventure with Nevin, Stefani, and Trevis. They provided not only an opportunity to remain close to my children but served as a welcome reprieve from my normally hectic life.

CHAPTER THIRTY-FIVE

The trips I took with my children to Mexico, Canada, and Europe had all been scheduled around their interests and needs. Then, in 1973, I began traveling with my friend Gertrude Davis Chern.

I had met Trudy when we were both members of the State Bar Family Law Committee, and we became good friends immediately. Trudy was ten years older, and she practiced law in Santa Maria, California, with two male lawyers she had recruited.

On our first trip together, Stefani and Trudy's husband, Dan, accompanied us. We stayed in a flat in the eastern part of London for more than two weeks while attending concerts and museums. We also walked and walked and walked. Our longest trip on foot took us from Bermondsey (across the street from the Tower of London) to the London Zoo. Both Dan and Stefani declined that adventure. The ten-mile jaunt left Trudy and me exhausted, but the experience was worth the effort.

Stefani took a side trip to Paris by herself to visit her cousin. I felt a little apprehensive about her traveling alone, but she had demonstrated her competency for traveling safely quite early in life.

Just before we all left England, we realized none of us had been to Liverpool. Trudy and Stefani did not feel compelled to remedy that, but Dan and I wanted to see the city. So, we took the train to Liverpool and returned within one day.

My first vacation with Trudy was so successful that we did a lot more foreign travel, generally to London or other English-speaking areas. We wanted to learn about the judicial system in other countries, but we could seldom find trials of interest other than rape prosecutions.

It was a special area of interest for us because at that time in the United States, the jury instruction for a rape case included this caution: "A charge (of rape) is easily made, and once made is hard to defend against; therefore, you should view the prosecutrix with caution." In the 1970s, members of Queen's Bench had won a petition in the California Supreme Court to eliminate that instruction.

We found that women were much better regarded in other parts of the world than in our country. In London, a man had been charged with rape after he invited a former girlfriend to lunch at his home. She said he did not provide lunch but raped her instead. In Canada, a defendant had refused to pay a prostitute after she performed her services. We were astonished that the cases tended to slant toward women. In fact, in only one country did the manner of prosecution resemble that seen in California.

Even when we didn't find an intriguing case to check out, we encountered much to keep us entertained. One of our most memorable trips to Europe took place immediately after the iron curtain had risen, which allowed eastern Europe to be free from Russian occupation. We traveled second class on that trip in a couchette, which featured six bunk-like beds in one train car.

We asked a woman we met on the train going to Budapest about how her country had managed before the iron curtain lifted. She had quite a bit to say, but it boiled down to how untenable it had been.

Almost no one spoke English in Budapest. We managed to get around due to Trudy's near-fluent Yiddish. Prague was not far away, and we spent a delightful day there.

On another trip, Trudy and I traveled to the northeast part of England to meet with a woman who had provided me with her PhD work to quote in my dissertation. She said the type of graduate work she did was difficult because the law librarians would allow her to view only one page at a time. We also met with a male psychologist in Canada whose work I had included in my dissertation.

Generally, however, Trudy and I participated in local walking trips in places near London. The trips were at least ten miles long, and our American couch-potato habits made the walks hard for us. Nevertheless, they were an outstanding part of our lives.

On one occasion, Trudy said someone at home asked why she continued to work when she was well into her seventies.

She replied, "I need to pay for the taxi from Heathrow to London and back."

CHAPTER THIRTY-SIX

Trevis graduated early from high school in 1978, at the age of sixteen. He wanted to attend medical school but did not want to put up with four years of college—in California or anywhere else in the United States. He had visited Nicaragua with a friend a year or so previously and had become fluent in Spanish, so he enrolled in medical school in Guadalajara. The family of one of his dad's friends offered him a place to live while he attended school there.

He moved to Guadalajara six months before his first medical school term started, and I was apprehensive about his being there on his own. After a few weeks, I decided to check on him.

If I were going to a foreign country, perhaps to rescue my son, I would need to be in the best physical and emotional condition possible. It seemed wise for me to cut alcohol out of my consumables. I did not have another drink, not even wine or champagne, for another two years. Floyd had stopped drinking in 1977, so I knew he would be comfortable with my abstinence. There was no fanfare, no dramatic announcement, no visits to Alcoholics Anonymous, and no communication to anyone about it. I simply stopped.

Trevis met me at the airport and hailed a taxi. He told the driver he was studying Spanish *privado* so he could attend medical school there. The driver dropped us at the place where Trevis was staying, and I felt comfortable with the house and the family. They all spoke English and treated us with great hospitality. I returned home within a few days, satisfied that my son was all right.

The next time I talked to Trevis, he said he had a temperature of 104 degrees. I did not understand why he could not find a doctor. I told him to put an ice compress on his forehead to bring the temperature down, advice that was soundly rejected by everyone with whom he spoke. However, he followed my instructions and soon recovered. That experience dampened his enthusiasm about attending medical school in Guadalajara. After his bicycle was stolen, he called and told me he was coming home because Mexico hadn't worked for him.

I didn't hear from Trevis for several days after that conversation, so I called Sherwin. His Mexican friend described how customs works in that country. The US returnee (especially someone as young as Trevis) must go through several "stations" at the airport check-in.

At each station, he would be expected to produce one set of papers for approval and one peso. The papers would be returned to him without the peso. He would have to repeat the same activity at the next station. Trevis had made several tries without the peso at each station, and he gave up after he was rejected. Eventually, he took enough pesos with him to reach the other side of the check-in process and board the airplane.

Since medical school in Mexico hadn't worked for him, Trevis focused on becoming an engineer like his paternal grandfather. He enrolled in the Colorado School of Mines in Golden, Colorado, near Denver. There, he visited his maternal grandmother, whom he had not previously known. Trevis visited her on a Sunday about once a month, and the two of them became close.

Mother had loaned me money for Stefani to attend college, with the provision that the loan would be forgiven if she graduated, which she did. When my mother learned that Trevis planned to attend the College of Mines, she loaned me an additional $5,000 at a low interest rate.

After Sherwin gave up his medical practice, he invested in a number of other business ventures, including real estate in the California mountains. Trevis returned home after his first year at Colorado Mines and joined his father's surveying group in those mountains. Nevin and one of Trevis's college friends became a part of the group as well.

On July 14, 1983, when Trevis was alone, he tried to attach a marker to the next spot, but there was nothing there. He stepped into empty space and fell two hundred feet to his death. None of us could accurately reconstruct his thinking to understand how he had reached the point of no return without realizing it. We speculated that he had been so focused on what he was doing that he did not comprehend the danger. Trevis was just three weeks short of his twenty-first birthday.

Sherwin chartered a private plane to fly to the location and asked Stefani to join him. They left about four o'clock in the afternoon. When they arrived, Sherwin said to her, "We've lost him."

Stefani and Trevis were as close as twins, and I don't know that she—or I—has ever recovered from his death.

Sherwin called Floyd to give us the tragic news. I hadn't planned to drive to San Francisco that night, but Floyd insisted that I be with him, so I conceded. When he told me about Trevis, I said I did not believe him. It couldn't be possible. Floyd told me to wake him at any time if I needed him. I stayed awake all night. My mind couldn't make sense of what had happened.

We held a memorial service a few days later. It took me about a week to absorb the enormity of the occasion. When I returned to my office a week later, everyone I met expressed their sympathy. One of my witnesses, a psychologist, summed it up by saying, "Death of a child is generationally inappropriate."

Somehow, I was able to continue all matters scheduled in my law practice. Perhaps I was still in shock.

I have three pictures of my children, ages five months to seven years, that hang in my bathroom. In another room, Trevis peeks around other pictures and appears to be hugging Nevin. I see Trevis every day.

His death devastated me. I failed to pursue my opportunity for a possible appointment to the bench as a judge. An applicant for the bench must spend many hours working on her application, obtaining recommendations, and practicing interviews. I felt so numb after Trevis's death that I could not manage to properly present the application.

Floyd had always supported me in my quest for the bench, but he didn't believe I was suited for the position. He was right. I respond negatively to being told what to do, and I cannot sit still and listen to hours of testimony, much of which I would have presented differently.

I don't regret ending my pursuit of a judgeship, but I've never gotten over the death of my youngest child. I doubt I ever will.

CHAPTER THIRTY-SEVEN

Stefani finished high school in 1978 and spent a summer in accelerated English at Menlo College. She and a professor there became romantically involved. After attending the University of California at Santa Barbara for one year, she moved to San Francisco. Her professor boyfriend had convinced her to attend the University of San Francisco and live with him.

After two years in San Francisco, where she attended art school, Stefi moved back in with me and earned her Bachelor of Arts in illustration. She had high hopes for a career as an artist but discovered that she needed an agent to compete in the art world. Landing an agent proved to be much more difficult than we had foreseen, so Stefani drove a taxi in San Francisco while earning a certificate in accounting.

I brought her into my office to deposit checks and do simple bookkeeping. On one occasion, my secretary unexpectedly gave herself a vacation. Stefi looked over the work to be done, did it efficiently, and earned the job as my new secretary.

After Nevin graduated from college, he came to live with me while he worked on his master's degree in earth sciences, a branch of geology. When he could not find a job he liked immediately after graduation, he moved to Canada to work on a project Sherwin had started.

Floyd retired from the real estate business in early 2000 just before I felt ready to retire from my law practice. While on a trip to Oregon, we decided to marry and came home via Reno, Nevada, where we obtained a license and a clergyman and said our vows on March 31, 2000. We bought a house in Sacramento, and I commuted to and from San Mateo.

While I worked in San Mateo, Floyd was alone in Sacramento with nothing to do. We learned that an excellent jewelry school offered courses a few miles from our house, so he enrolled and became a goldsmith and bench jeweler. After I retired, we began taking trips to the Northwest to sell his creations.

During a trip to Seattle in 2002, we had just finished a day exhibiting at a gem show. Floyd went into the bedroom, lay down on our bed, and died. There was no excitement in a hospital, no fanfare, and no drama. He was just gone. His death left me in a world I did not understand without him by my side.

My cousin, who resided in Cheney, Washington, joined me in Seattle and drove me home. I sold the motor home and the house in Sacramento and then returned to my house in Foster City, where Stefi still lived.

In 2004, she decided to spend time with people other than family, so she moved to Marin County, where she lived with a group of young people for the next several years.

In the meantime, Sherwin had acquired a reputation for treating people badly, including Nevin. After a significant betrayal by his father, Nevin left Canada and returned to Marin County, where he married his first wife.

I felt so proud of him for making the decision to move back to California. When something did not go well for me, or if someone in the family treated me poorly, I left, even though it meant terminating the relationship. Nevin had either inherited or absorbed the same ability to improve his life. He and his second wife, Rebecca (a great lady), raised two boys successfully, and he was successful in business as well.

Sherwin died on July 20, 2008, the day of Mother's and Betty's birthday, but he and I had parted ways long before that day.

CHAPTER THIRTY-EIGHT

Mother and I reconciled completely many years before her death in 1992 at the age of eighty-nine. It didn't happen suddenly but rather evolved gradually over decades. After she appeared at our door in 1961, I heard from my aunt that Mother had fallen and been hospitalized for an extended time.

My mother told me her doctor had left dye in her spinal cord so he could monitor any changes. A case in California had returned a substantial verdict for the plaintiff in a case involving similar facts. Colorado was still of the opinion that doctors do not sue other doctors, so the physician that mistreated my mother escaped with no responsibility for what (to me) was obvious malpractice. She experienced constant pain for the last decades of her life and could walk only with the assistance of elaborate braces.

Although she and I had not fully reconciled at that point, I flew to Denver and visited Mother when my father was not at home. She came to see me in Foster City three times. Her first visit, in 1982, coincided with Nevin's offer to put a new roof on my house. He had hired Trevis to help him, so they both got to spend time with their grandmother.

I do not know how Mother managed to maintain her relationship with Dad, but I was happy for her that she could do so. My relationship with him proved to be a struggle.

Dad was another animal. I thought we might reconcile at the wedding of one of Betty's daughters. Unfortunately, her first daughter married in 1984 when I was studying for the comprehensive examination for my LLM (Master of Laws) tax course. I had approached that project by attending and participating in class but doing little or no outside studying. I had to pass the final, so I could not afford the time to attend the wedding.

My next opportunity to reconnect came with my sister Anne's wedding. I called Dad and asked him if I could attend the event. He said bluntly, "You have ruined my life." Despite that inauspicious beginning, we got through the conversation, and a wedding invitation appeared. The fact that it especially excluded Sherwin made it clear that Dad had not forgotten or forgiven him for his role in the situation. Stefani was eight years old at the time. She appeared to be acceptable and thus was allowed to attend the nuptials.

We were seated conspicuously far away from the rest of the family. We were able to greet Dad only by standing behind him while he talked to someone else and then jumping in front of him as soon as he was free. Our reception was quite chilly, and I cried most of that night.

When Betty's younger daughter married, I asked Betty directly if we could attend. She said, "Yes." We arrived the evening before the bachelor dinner and joined Mother and Dad at Betty's house. We spent the time discussing the relative merits of John Brodie, quarterback for the Denver Broncos, and Joe Montana, quarterback for the San Francisco Forty-Niners.

After our return home, Dad wrote me a note saying he was happy that the "tension between us" had subsided. I felt the same way. I visited Dad just before Mother died, and he asked if I would attend her funeral. That time I took Nevin with me, as Dad had not yet met him. Dad said to Nevin, "Wasn't your father a Jew?" Nevin didn't reply and had no interest in seeing him again.

I knew then that my father was unable to put his animosity about my marriage to Sherwin to rest. So be it.

A few days before Dad died, Anne called and said that if I wanted to see him again, I should do so immediately. I flew to Denver, rented a car, and drove to Dad's house. I apologized to him for my participation in "this whole thing."

I do not know whether my father heard or understood me, but he did not respond.

EPILOGUE

In 2003, about a year after Floyd's death, I married Ronald Borden. We had been good friends since we met in 1971 at a party for new members of the San Mateo Private Defender group. Ron thought for himself, as I did. He had also been married twice, and he was a pro-choice Republican, which suited me perfectly. Ron even read my entire dissertation, or at least he convinced me he had.

We traveled together frequently and set a goal to visit all fifty-two states in our country. We drove to the Northwest for Ron and visited Washington, Oregon, Idaho, Wyoming, and Nevada. My trip took us east to Missouri, Kentucky, West Virginia, and Virginia. We also traveled to Washington, DC, took a weeklong trip by airplane to Alaska, and visited New York at least twice a year for art auctions. On one occasion, we drove through New England and detoured through Pennsylvania on our return to New York.

Ron had Asperger's disease, which made it difficult for him to interact well with other people. Nevertheless, we enjoyed an untroubled relationship until his first stroke in 2015, when he became less loving and generally more disagreeable.

We made concessions to each other after that time. In late 2015, he flew to the Philippines for his own personal activities while I traveled to Cuernavaca to spend two weeks studying Spanish and attempting to become fluent in the language. I nearly succeeded in learning Spanish, and I certainly learned a lot about Mexico.

After Ron's stroke, he wanted me to spend most of my time doing nothing, because *he* did nothing. That was not for me. I found idleness boring. Instead, I gathered information from my law practice and my dissertation and wrote two novels, *Susannah, A Lawyer: From Tragedy to Triumph*, and *Perfect Clarity: A Novel about our Male-Dominated Misogynist Society and Four Women Who Fought Back (1874 to the Present)*.

Ron had a second stroke in 2016 and never fully recovered. His illnesses and his death in 2018 took a toll on me. After he died, I moved to a retirement home in Marin County, which gave me the opportunity to spend meaningful time with my children and two grandchildren.

POSTCRIPT

When my brother and I met for the first time after many years apart, his wife said the purported anti-Semitic response our parents displayed was trivial. If my parents' reaction had not been due to their discovery that Sherwin was Jewish, the reason for their behavior must have been something else. But no one has ever discovered what truly caused their outrageous objections to my marriage.

My brother asked, "Was it worth what it cost you?"

The answer is a resounding yes! Although I feel as if I spent twenty years in a boxing ring, I could not let my parents, my husband, or anyone else live my life for me. If my parents (or anyone else) would not allow me to be *me*, I had no option other than to rescue myself.

My father had chosen an unusual profession, as psychiatry was uncommon in the 1930s. He became a leader in the development of psychiatry as part of a doctor's medical education. My mother's career choice was even more extraordinary. For a married woman to earn a PhD and become an executive in a large medical establishment was inconceivable in 1935, but she did it.

Grandmother and Grandfather Rymer had also bucked society. Few couples had the vision and determination to build their own home by dismantling an existing house many miles away and carting every piece across the state. And just imagine living and raising your children in the mountains while trying to find gold there. That had been the Reinhardt way.

Change and rebellion against society were embedded in my family history, so my marriage to someone "not of my faith" should not have been unexpected. I had come from a family of unconventional individuals, people with resilience. If something did not work for us or authorities challenged us, we did not wilt and die. We stepped aside and tried something else until we found a way that worked. We are a people who have always chosen our own lifestyle.

My choice was not rebellion, but I felt compelled to do what suited me. I had to become who I wanted to be. Certainly, I could never have accommodated my father's intellectually dishonest, untrue, crazy idea of who he expected me to be.

Because I saw no other alternative, I chose to embrace the quality of resilience.

And so it was that in 2008, the year I turned seventy-seven, Queen's Bench honored me with their Lifetime Achievement Award. That honor meant more to me than any prior accomplishment. Receiving it confirmed that my entire life, including every effort and struggle, had been worthwhile. Resilience had help me overcome each challenge and achieve my goals, including the goal of freeing women from a legal system that prevented us from becoming our true selves.

From the dawn of humanity, men have dominated women, often threatening our safety, sanity, and very lives. By the 1960s, our society no longer sanctioned those behaviors. It was my great honor and privilege to help lead us (we as women) out of the darkness of subjugation into the light of equality and joy.

So, was it worth what it cost me? Of course it was.

Of course.

ABOUT THE AUTHOR

S hortly after passing the bar on her fortieth birthday, Ruth Rymer noticed that female attorneys were not treated as well as their male counterparts in the practice of law. This observation inspired her to advocate for women's rights throughout her legal career in the Bay Area.

Her roles as President of Queen's Bench and the NorCal Chapter of the American Academy of Matrimonial Lawyers would contribute to her training for statewide leadership.

In 1977, Ruth chaired the commission that established family law as a certified specialty in California, making family law a more respectable practice for attorneys. *The Best Lawyers in America* listed her from 1988 until the year 2000 when she retired.

Before practicing law, Ruth earned her Graduate Gemologist degree from Gemological Institute of America. Today she still enjoys working with jewelry and gifting it as party favors.

Ruth has two grown children and has survived the loss of a child. Her publications include a lay text and three books: *California Divorce: Through the Legal Maze*, the historical novel *Susannah, A Lawyer: From Tragedy to Triumph*; *Perfect Clarity: A Novel about Our Male-Dominated Misogynist Society and Four Women Who Fought Back (1874 to the Present)*; and *Raising the Bar: A Lawyer's Memoir*.

www.ruthrymer.com